Association for Scottish
Schools & Further Educ

**This book is to be returned on or before
the last date stamped below.**

SCOTTISH
COLLECTION

809
3
TRE

Falkirk Council

Dr James McGonigal
Ronald Renton
Lorna Borrowman Smith

First published in Great Britain, 2003
by the Association for Scottish Literary Studies
Department of Scottish History
9 University Gardens
University of Glasgow
Glasgow G12 8QH

British Library Cataloguing in Publication Data
A CIP record for this book is available from the
British Library

ISBN 0 948877 55 3

We thank Duncan Jones for his inventiveness in planning the structure of this
work. We are also grateful to Dr Margaret Renton for valuable IT assistance,
and to Wendy Axford of the School Library Association in Scotland for
suggesting possible sources of texts.

We very much regret that our friend and colleague Alistair Chynoweth,
Principal Teacher of English at the High School of Dundee, did not live to
see this publication to whose progress he contributed so willingly.
Treasure Islands is dedicated to Alistair's memory.

The Association for Scottish Literary Studies acknowledges
the support of the Scottish Arts Council towards the
publication of this book.

CONTENTS

INTRODUCTION

The Association for Scottish Literary Studies has produced this short critical guide for parents, teachers, students, librarians, publishers, booksellers and all who wish young people to enjoy Scottish stories of good quality. The compiling group have wide experience in encouraging the use of fiction in schools and we believe strongly that imaginative reading should contribute to the basic education of all young people in their later primary and early secondary stages. This principle is already expressed in the Scottish Executive Education Department's National Guidelines on English Language 5–14.

But even without the claims of the curriculum we know that there is sheer, often subversive, pleasure to be had from personal reading at all ages. This is a satisfaction which is difficult to pin down and has nothing necessarily to do with formal schooling, but it has endured, and although it shows little sign of capitulating to the power of contemporary electronic media, it merits all the support it can get. We have therefore taken it upon ourselves to suggest some fiction which is likely to be attractive to 10–14 year olds.

For the most part, the 160 books that we recommend have been written specifically with a youthful readership in mind. At the same time we fully recognise that as readers develop in confidence and curiosity they will cross and re-cross the open frontiers of so-called Children's, Young Adult and Adult fiction, sometimes quite precociously preferring grown-up writing. This is a good sign that the reading habit is becoming addictive. Conversely we should record as compilers that we have immensely enjoyed the reading we have undertaken for this survey. It seems that it is never too late for parents and adults generally to seek out again the pleasures of Scottish books for young people.

The title of our guide, *Treasure Islands*, is a reminder that Scotland has long had a memorable place on the world map of children's literature. In their very different ways writers such as Sir Walter Scott, R.M. Ballantyne, George MacDonald, Andrew Lang, R.L. Stevenson and J.M. Barrie are widely recognised to have been seminal influences in its development. We are keen therefore that our young readers should have a chance to explore the wealth of classic and contemporary Scottish writing that is, or could be, available to them. We have no wish to be parochial or to exclude other sources of good fiction but we consider that our selected Scottish texts have something distinctive and valuable to offer in matters such as history, social issues, landscape and language.

As far as we know, this is the first survey of its kind and we are convinced that it comes not a moment too soon. Regrettably many of our recommended books are now hard to find: often they have fallen out of print and are in danger of being completely forgotten. At present there is also a dearth of critical advice on Scottish children's fiction. The books on which we comment are simply a thoughtful choice from a much greater range to which young readers in Scotland are entitled to have access. We hope that publishers will bring some of these back into circulation, that a way can be found nationally to keep a core selection continuously in print, and that university faculties of arts and education will view Scottish children's literature as a domain likely to reward further investigation.

Mostly, but not exclusively, the books that we list have been written for young people in the 10–14 age range. Some have skilfully kept the needs of less confident readers in mind. They tend to be located in Scotland or use Scottish topics or characters, and to be the work of authors born and/or living in Scotland. The majority are novels, but collections of short stories and traditional tales are also included. A number have Scots language forms but Gaelic is present only in translation. Users of the Guide will of course notice exceptions to these generalisations. Most notably our recommendations are enriched by a significant number of writers who are not Scots but use Scotland for settings. We have also been happy to lay claim to works by writers such as Anne Fine and J.K. Rowling on nothing more than their residential qualifications, past or present. There is a wide representation of authors, some of whom have earned multiple entries. We should underline that our sampling may not represent the whole diversity of a writer's work, and that the differences in totals do not necessarily indicate our views on relative merits among authors.

In dates of publication our choices run from 1824 to 2003, with the emphasis falling naturally on more recent writing. Some of our older titles can seem irretrievably time-bound, their language, attitudes and assumptions being so alien to today's young readers that they may be rejected out of hand. These earlier texts are often more leisurely in pace, more complex in syntax and vocabulary, seemingly slower and more wordy. By contrast contemporary works appear to be stripped down, informal, and more direct. They are often much shorter. But who is to legislate confidently on the appeal of fiction? Happily there is no accounting for the tastes of individual young readers once they are hooked on books, as witness the popularity of recent lengthy and complex offerings by writers such as Philip Pullman.

About the apparent imbalances within our selection we can only say that these reflect what was available to us. We do not regard them as weaknesses, although it is interesting to speculate how they have come about. They include the predominance of historical topics; uneven regional coverage; the popularity of the Highlands for middle-class summer holiday adventures; and the choice of Scotland as a preferred location for supernatural events, monsters, witchcraft and fantasy. We have chosen several fine attempts to explore contemporary urban settings and difficult social issues. For some reason however we do not have a single novel dealing centrally with football. Sport is indeed the smallest category in our survey.

In schools the days are long past when fiction for younger students was confined to being the staple fodder for class and home readers and the testing that accompanied them. Nowadays we hope that stories such as those we recommend can be used in much more attractive ways to contribute to Primary language work or the Secondary English syllabus. They may for example serve as stimuli for students' own writing; sources for dramatic activities; topics for talks, group or class discussions; supports for thematic study (history, environment, social issues); or texts for close reading and developing awareness of the writer's craft. But most importantly of all, the books we have listed should be seen as personal enjoyment for the young individual reader and need not become part of school work at all.

We have already suggested that it is often difficult nowadays to locate Scottish fiction for young people. However there are useful sources of guidance. Scottish Book Trust, the School Library Association in Scotland and the public library service are able to help in finding and using Scottish materials. Some bookshops have children's sections which carry work by the better known Scottish authors. Individual schools and libraries may also make recommendations.

A great deal of information can moreover be obtained via the Internet. Authors have their own websites and some societies exist to celebrate the achievements of well known writers. Out-of-print texts can frequently be picked up quite cheaply via websites such as abebooks.co.uk and amazon.co.uk. There are also sites devoted exclusively to children's fiction. Several of our more popular titles can be supported by audio books and by videos based on film versions of the originals.

Scottish Book Trust's Writers in Scotland Scheme lists writers for children who are willing to visit schools, libraries and other groups to talk about their work. Finally we are fortunate in Scotland that every August the hugely successful Edinburgh International Book Festival presents children's and schools' programmes which offer young people the excitement of meeting in person a galaxy of contemporary authors and their most recent books.

1. The entry for each text outlines the setting of the story, its plot and main characters. It says something about themes and offers an appreciative comment; it also suggests the age range within which the work is most likely to be of interest, and its level of reading demand for that range. The compiling group is convinced that all of the chosen works are worth introducing to young readers. We emphasise however that each entry is a statement by one member of the group, and not a consensus verdict by committee. Personal differences in attitude and style are therefore to be expected.

2. For convenience of reference we have arranged our notes into categories according to our judgements of the type of text. We are well aware that it is not possible to do this with much precision since category names are largely arbitrary and tend moreover to overlap. One novel can be a historical horror story, another a humorous fantasy, and yet another an animal story about a hunted outsider. Nonetheless we have thought it helpful on balance to arrange our notes in the following groupings: **Adventure; Animals; Family; Growing up; History; Humour; Love; Mystery; Outsiders; Science Fiction & Fantasy; Short stories; Sport; Supernatural & Horror; Thrillers; Traditional stories.**

3. We have also supplied some keywords as a quick summary for each text. We have made very rough-and-ready suggestions about the likely interest and age range of each work within the years 10–14. Again we do this tentatively in the knowledge that it is rash to generalise about the types of texts likely to be psychologically best suited to any stage of development.

4. As further guidance, we have identified for each age range 3 broad reading levels suggesting linguistic demand:

- texts which in their language are likely to be immediately accessible to readers in the indicated age range,

- those which are likely to be reasonably straightforward for readers in that range,

- those which are likely to be more demanding for readers in that range.

These levels are the most problematic of our codings. Experienced teachers are wary of such indicators for they know that if young people alight upon a text dealing with something that interests them, they are willing to persevere at a level that stretches and extends their reading skills. We recognise also that skilled reading aloud can make difficult texts more accessible to insecure readers.

5. We have provided indexes by title, author and type of text.

6. The publication details in each note are, we believe, accurate up to June 2003. Wherever possible these include the date of the first edition and the ISBN of the most recent edition, whether that is currently available, or out of print *(op)*.

AN INVITATION TO READERS OF ALL AGES

We are well aware that our selection of fiction is not yet comprehensive, and we hope to expand it by adding new entries to *Treasure Islands* on the website of the Association for Scottish Literary Studies. If you have favourite Scottish novels or selections of stories which you would like to recommend to young readers, we shall be delighted to consider adding them to our collection. You might care to submit your suggestions using the format of the present entries in this volume.

The e-mail address is: **treasureislands@asls.org.uk**

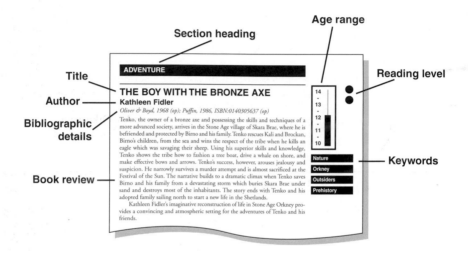

Section heading

Age range

Reading level

Title

Author

Bibliographic details

Book review

Keywords

ADVENTURE

THE BOY WITH THE BRONZE AXE
Kathleen Fidler
Oliver & Boyd, 1968 (op); Puffin, 1986, ISBN:0140305637 (op)

Tenko, the owner of a bronze axe and possessing the skills and techniques of a more advanced society, arrives in the Stone Age village of Skara Brae, where he is befriended and protected by Birno and his family. Tenko rescues Kali and Brockan, Birno's children, from the sea and wins the respect of the tribe when he kills an eagle which was savaging their sheep. Using his superior skills and knowledge, Tenko shows the tribe how to fashion a tree boat, drive a whale on shore, and make effective bows and arrows. Tenko's success, however, arouses jealousy and suspicion. He narrowly survives a murder attempt and is almost sacrificed at the Festival of the Sun. The narrative builds to a dramatic climax when Tenko saves Birno and his family from a devastating storm which buries Skara Brae under sand and destroys most of the inhabitants. The story ends with Tenko and his adopted family sailing north to start a new life in the Shetlands.

Kathleen Fidler's imaginative reconstruction of life in Stone Age Orkney provides a convincing and atmospheric setting for the adventures of Tenko and his friends.

14
-
13
-
12
-
11
-
10

Nature
Orkney
Outsiders
Prehistory

THE BOY WITH THE BRONZE AXE

Kathleen Fidler

Oliver & Boyd, 1968 (op); Puffin, 1986, ISBN:0140305637 (op)

Tenko, the owner of a bronze axe and possessing the skills and techniques of a more advanced society, arrives in the Stone Age village of Skara Brae, where he is befriended and protected by Birno and his family. Tenko rescues Kali and Brockan, Birno's children, from the sea and wins the respect of the tribe when he kills an eagle which was savaging their sheep. Using his superior skills and knowledge, Tenko shows the tribe how to fashion a tree boat, drive a whale on shore, and make effective bows and arrows. Tenko's success, however, arouses jealousy and suspicion. He narrowly survives a murder attempt and is almost sacrificed at the Festival of the Sun. The narrative builds to a dramatic climax when Tenko saves Birno and his family from a devastating storm which buries Skara Brae under sand and destroys most of the inhabitants. The story ends with Tenko and his adopted family sailing north to start a new life in the Shetlands.

Kathleen Fidler's imaginative reconstruction of life in Stone Age Orkney provides a convincing and atmospheric setting for the adventures of Tenko and his friends.

```
14
-
13
-
12
-
11
-
10
```

Nature

Orkney

Outsiders

Prehistory

THE CORAL ISLAND

R.M. Ballantyne

Thomas Nelson & Sons, 1857 (op); Puffin Classics (abridged), 1994, ISBN:0140367616

The Coral Island, an account of three young castaways' adventures during the first half of the nineteenth century among the coral islands of the Pacific, is a classic of its genre. Ralph the Rover, Jack Martin and Peterkin Gay are washed up on a deserted island after a disastrous storm. Resourceful, inventive and determined, they quickly adapt to life in their Pacific Eden with the minimum of angst. The story, narrated by Ralph, describes the boys' adventure on the island, his experiences as a captive on a pirate ship, his return to the coral island and the boys' subsequent mission to rescue Avatea, a Samoan girl. With Jack as leader they find food, make tools, build a boat, explore the island and find evidence of a previous lonely inhabitant. The narrative is packed with incident and the author's descriptions of the boys' submarine garden, the shark attack, the water spouts and the subterranean 'diamond' cave are memorable. The story acknowledges the uneasy alliance between Christianity and trade but does not question it. Its lasting power lies in the author's ability to combine the staple ingredients of castaway tales into a coherent narrative and his meticulous use of his knowledge of the South Seas to recreate its beauties and its terrors for the reader.

```
14
-
13
-
12
-
11
-
10
```

History

Nature

Pirates

Seafaring

Shipwreck

South Seas

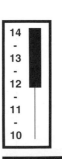

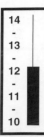

14
-
13
-
12
-
11
-
10

Aberdeen

History

Mystery

Poverty

DANGER BY GASLIGHT

Eileen Ramsay

Scottish Children's Press, 1998, ISBN:1899827838

This novel incorporates painlessly some social history concerning the lives of deprived children in the heart of Victorian Aberdeen. Jamie has no father, Mam scrapes a living as a mill worker, and they live in grinding poverty as lodgers. School is freezing in winter, smelly in summer, and its routines are severe. Harry the wise and daft street urchin sleeping rough does not go to school at all. But there are compensations: the excitement of sliding in winter, of the traditional Timmer Market in summer, and of visits to the theatre and the new public library. Stock characters such as teachers, the janitor and the local policeman are lightly sketched. Underlying Jamie's adventures is the traditional motif of the clever lad who overcomes dangers to discover his unexpected birthright. Running errands for a luxury grocer, Jamie gains entry to the household of a wealthy Aberdeen advocate. Thereafter danger looms as a lurking enemy tries to frighten him off or even destroy him. The mystery is finally solved in the granite depths of the huge Rubislaw Quarry.

14
-
13
-
12
-
11
-
10

Canada

Clearances

Emigration

Highlands

History

THE DESPERATE JOURNEY

Kathleen Fidler

Lutterworth Press, 1964 (op); Floris Kelpies, 2002, ISBN:0863154018

Evicted by Patrick Sellar from their croft in Culmailie in Sutherland, the Murray family travel to Glasgow to begin a new life. Sickened by the squalor and brutality of life in the slums and mills of Glasgow, they seize the opportunity to settle in Canada on land bought by the Earl of Selkirk from the Hudson's Bay Company. The central characters, David and Kirsty Murray, witness the evictions and the burning of the crofters' homes; endure the hardships of child labour in a Glasgow cotton mill; survive the Atlantic crossing on a disease-ridden ship, and witness bitter feuding among rival colonists. Kathleen Fidler's well-paced narrative skilfully conveys the Murrays' epic journey and the historical settings are convincingly portrayed. The wide scope of the story does not allow for much psychological development, but David and Kirsty Murray are spirited and resilient characters who engage the interest and sympathy of the reader.

EMMA TUPPER'S DIARY
Peter Dickinson

Gollancz, 1971 (op); Puffin, 1973, ISBN:0140305912 (op)

'The McAndrews played to hurt.'

Emma from Botswana is holidaying on the Highland estate of her wealthy McAndrew cousins whom she has not previously met. The setting is a remote lochside in Morar. Are there monsters in the loch? This funny and intellectually challenging novel is at first sight another Ransome-type outdoors adventure complete with map and diagram and plausible technical details about how things work. However all is not as it seems. The wary Emma, who keeps a diary, gradually realises that her cousins are a brat pack of selfish snobs. Farce and near tragedy mingle in efforts made to resurrect an antiquated midget sub to search for the fabled monsters. The novel's strength lies in the interplay of awkward adolescent personalities as they wrestle with the Heath Robinsonish engineering of the submarine and the horrors of an underwater cave system. There are echoes of Prospero in the aging father of the McAndrew brood, a spy/biologist and sugar-daddy to the gorgeous shoplifting Miss Poop, who finally arrives for a family board meeting to resolve the fate of the vulnerable relict plesiosaurs.

14
13
12
11
10

Family

Highlands

Humour

Monsters

FUGITIVE
Cathy MacPhail

Puffin, 1999, ISBN:0140382712

Jack Tarrant is an only child who stays with his mother Rose. The novel starts humorously as his mother struggles to master a borrowed car and cons the cinema into letting Jack in for a child price. It continues in much the same vein as we meet Jack's school friends, including Spotty Lizzie, and they start to take part in the school musical, *Calamity Jane*. However, something is wrong at home. A police inspector has been calling Rose and Jack finds out more about his life, his mother and the police than he would ever have imagined. This is a good thriller with credible characters among both children and adults, and plenty of incident and sharp dialogue.

14
13
12
11
10

Crime

Family

Growing up

Outsiders

14
-
13
-
12
-
11
-
10

Crofting

Espionage

Heroism

Skye

THE HILL OF THE RED FOX
Allan Campbell McLean
Collins, 1955 (op); Floris Kelpies, 2002, ISBN:086241055X

The Ordinance Survey sheet of North Skye will be a stimulating aid to the reading of this novel, which has the same lovingly detailed location as McLean's later *The Master of Morgana*. It is an espionage thriller strongly influenced by *The Thirty-Nine Steps* and with tinges of the early Ian Fleming. Young Alastair's first summer holiday visit to his family croft starts with alarming encounters on the Glasgow to Mallaig train. When he reaches his inheritance on the moorland below Sgurr a' Mhadaidh Ruaidh he gradually realises that all is not well. Events uncover a plot to smuggle blackmailed atomic scientists to Russia. Masterminding the villainy is one of those chameleons who can on the hooding of an eye transform from amiable English gentleman into ruthless foreign agent. The story, which is mainly one of male fellowship and strength, climaxes violently in the self-sacrifice of Duncan Mor, a man of Fingalian heroic stature and character. The crofting environment is integral to the action, with sympathetic descriptions of communal activities such as peat gathering, mackerel fishing and sheep shearing.

14
-
13
-
12
-
11
-
10

Highlands

History

Jacobites

Seafaring

KIDNAPPED
Robert Louis Stevenson
Cassell, 1886 (op); Penguin, 2002, ISBN:0141439327

This powerful adventure novel exploits the possibilities of Scottish history and terrain for young readers. In 1751 David Balfour, an orphan, leaves his Borders home to seek his fortune, as directed by his late father, at the House of Shaws near Edinburgh. His frightened, conniving uncle has him kidnapped on board the brig *Covenant* bound for the Americas. On the voyage round Scotland treachery forces David into the company of Alan Breck Stewart, a proscribed Jacobite. Period and setting are skilfully evoked but Stevenson's focus is on plot and character, seen through David's eyes. A prim, sheltered lad, he finds himself brutally challenged by the grimness of his experiences on the *Covenant* and in his Highland wanderings when the ship founders. After the Appin murder he is locked into hurtful conflict with the flamboyant Alan during their hazardous flight south. A main theme is the clash between his Lowland prejudices and the ways of Gaels such as Cluny Macpherson and Robin Oig. In Edinburgh, as David gains his inheritance, what should be a happy ending is clouded by the looming consequences of the killing of the Red Fox, 'a cold gnawing in my inside like a remorse for something wrong'. These consequences unfold in *Catriona* (1893).

MASTER OF MORGANA
Allan Campbell McLean

Collins, 1960 (op); Canongate Kelpies, 1990, ISBN:0862412757

Like McLean's earlier *The Hill of the Red Fox* this thriller is set in the Lealt area of Skye. In the 1950s, before the Bridge came, the area is still isolated and the roads are poor. Niall, sixteen, lives on a croft with his young sister Morag and their widowed mother. Trouble starts when his older brother is injured in a mysterious accident on a bridge above the salmon bothy where he works. Sensing something wrong Niall visits the Factor and gets a summer job replacing his brother in the coble crew who lodge in the supposedly haunted bothy. What is Morgana and who is her Master? Central to the book is the relationship between Niall and the enigmatic John MacGregor, skipper of the coble. The author skilfully carries through to denouement parallels between MacGregor and Long John Silver, the ambivalent villain of *Treasure Island*. The story's crofting and fishing background is deftly handled, with compelling descriptions of the salmon netting. With confident older readers a possible approach is to explore this fast-moving novel in tandem with Stevenson's classic.

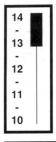

14
-
13
-
12
-
11
-
10

Crofting

Fishing

Mystery

Skye

ME AND MA GAL
Des Dillon

Argyll Publishing, 1995 (op); Review, 2001, ISBN:0747267065

This novel of industrial, working class childhood is set in Coatbridge, near Glasgow. It describes the adventures in a day in the lives of nine year old Derrick, the narrator, and his friend Gal. For these boys their recreation area is the local railway track, burn and sewer pipe. They taunt the railway police, hide daringly close to a passing train, go bird nesting (but are very careful not to damage eggs about to hatch), play dare-devilishly on the sewer pipe, trip up middle class golfers and have an encounter with a local 14-year-old tough guy who, afraid of being accused of hurting Derrick, buys them off with a gift of a knife and other items. The story climaxes with Strangler Joe, a disturbed adult, attacking and holding both boys until Gal succeeds in injuring him with the knife and securing their escape.

14
-
13
-
12
-
11
-
10

Coatbridge

Friendship

Scots language

This is a brilliantly observed and authentic evocation of childhood. It captures the mind and mannerisms of the growing boys – their swagger and *braggadocio* and their reticence and reluctance to show weakness in case of being thought 'soft'. The hero worship and indulgence in fantasy are exactly what one would expect from boys of that age. Urban Scots expression is very well handled and skilful use is made of typography to reinforce the events of the story. The novel, however, is a mature reflection on childhood and is suitable only for the upper end of the age range.

RIBBON OF FIRE
Allan Campbell McLean
Collins, 1962 (op); Floris Kelpies, 2002, ISBN:0863154107

In Skye in 1884 in the wake of the Highland Clearances the people are still in conflict with their landlords. 16-year-old Alasdair Stewart has been wrongfully accused of writing a letter threatening the life of the Laird, General Kemball-Denison. The real villain, however, is his factor. Unknown to his employer he has increased the tenants' rents hoping that they will rebel and thus give him the opportunity to evict them. After an exciting incident which results in Alasdair's father being rescued from prison by Lachlann Ban and some friends they have to take to the hills as outlaws. The notorious Sheriff Ivory calls in the marines. Lachlann Ban and his supporters prepare to resist them at a hill pass above their village but resistance melts when Alasdair tells them the full extent of Ivory's threats which he has learned from Fiona, the Laird's daughter. She and her father are decent people but even the Laird's improved conditions are not good enough for Lachlann Ban. This is a very exciting, thought-provoking story with moments of real suspense, particularly Alasdair's escape from a deep hole in the hillside by way of an underground channel.

A SOUND OF TRUMPETS
Allan Campbell McLean
Collins, 1967 (op); Canongate Kelpies, 1985, ISBN:0862410959 (op)

The sequel to McLean's *Ribbon of Fire*, this novel is also set on the north of Skye. The Laird who turned out to be a just man has died suddenly. His plans for Alasdair are thwarted by the unscrupulous factor, Major Traill, and, instead of an Edinburgh education, the boy is given a job as stable boy at the inn of the bullying tacksman Uilleam Mor. Here he learns of a scheme to evict an innocent widow. With the unexpected return of Lachlann Ban plans are hatched and local resistance mounted: the ground officer's stackyard is burned down, the inn's beer cellar is vandalised and one of the factor's officers is accidentally killed. Police and marines arrive. Lachlann and Alasdair and their friends try other bold tactics which are, however, ineffective in the long term.

The book has many thrilling escapades and marvellous descriptions of the resistance fighters' hideout high on Beinn Edra, but in the end the lesson to be learned is that the law is mightier than violence and the best way forward is to act within the law.

TREASURE ISLAND
Robert Louis Stevenson
Cassell, 1883 (op); Penguin Classics, 1994, ISBN:0140620834

This is one of the supreme fictions for confident young readers – a tale of 18th century pirates, villains and treasure maps. Jim Hawkins is a West Country lad who as a result of terrifying encounters in his mother's inn inherits a chart showing the way to buried loot on a remote island. He confides in the local doctor and squire who promptly buy a ship and recruit a captain and crew. With Jim as cabin boy the expedition optimistically sets sail from Bristol on its dangerous quest to the Caribbean. But trouble is stirring. Under the malign influence of Long John Silver, the one-legged cook, the crew mutinies on arrival at the island. The two factions battle to establish supremacy and claim the treasure. A struggle between good and evil, loyalty and betrayal, develops around the beguilingly ambiguous personality of Silver who seems at different times a reliable mentor, a merciless killer, and a lovable rogue. Hawkins recalls his own experiences as a boy alone in this treacherous adult world trying to identify who is to be trusted. His rapidly moving narrative, shot through with gleams of nightmarish horror, is much more powerful than any simple adventure yarn.

14
-
13
-
12
-
11
-
10

Horror

Pirates

Seafaring

Treasure

ANIMALS

14
-
13
-
12
-
11
-
10

Borders

Dogs

Farming

Growing up

Humour

FLASH THE SHEEPDOG
Kathleen Fidler
Lutterworth Press, 1965 (op); Floris Kelpies, 1989, ISBN:0862410711

After his sister leaves for America to get married, Tom Stokes, an orphan, goes to live with his aunt and uncle on a sheep farm in the Scottish Borders until his sister is settled in her new home. Homesick for London and intimidated by his uncle's strong personality, he finds it hard at first to adjust to the life of the farm. Gifted a pup by a neighbouring farmer, Tom sets out to train the animal as a sheepdog. Taught by his uncle, who gradually warms to his London nephew, Tom masters the art of sheepdog training and, helped by his friend Elspeth, wins the local sheepdog trials. A dog dealer offers to buy Flash, but Tom refuses to sell him and finally chooses to live permanently with his aunt and uncle.

The technicalities of sheepdog training and the suspense of the trials are conveyed in an accessible and entertaining manner and Tom and Flash's adventures in the fog and the rescuing of the sheep in the winter storm create dramatic tension. The characters of his uncle and aunt are presented with warmth and humour and the rural setting is convincingly portrayed.

14
-
13
-
12
-
11
-
10

Adventure

Farming

Forth valley

Foxes

Mystery

FOX FARM
Eileen Dunlop
Oxford University Press, 1978 (op); Canongate Kelpies, 1987, ISBN:0862411343 (op)

Set during the Second World War, this novel starts out as a conventional animal adventure. Two boys, Richard son of a farmer and Alan fostered from the city, are not particularly close friends but after the farmer kills a vixen they agree to share in the secret survival of a fox cub they have found. The need not to tell the adults leads them into secret thefts and into strange hiding places on other land off the farm. The story is complicated by an ancient curse visited upon a neighbouring farm owned by the Fauxes and this is linked to the non-return of one of the family from the war. Eileen Dunlop is too shrewd a writer to make the links simplistic and the boys learn that their imaginings and fears are in a context of real people living in a pressurised world. This reality includes their awareness of each other. The physical location, on the banks of the River Forth, plays a large part in creating the atmosphere. Readers can appreciate that this is the author's own favourite among her stories because it recreates the world of her own childhood.

GREAT NORTHERN?
Arthur Ransome
Jonathan Cape, 1947 (op); Red Fox, 2001, ISBN:0099964007

Ransome's last novel and the only one to take place in Scotland, this archetypal summer adventure is set in the thirties but has a contemporary theme of conservation. Eight Swallows and Amazons are cruising the Minch when they happen upon the first nest site of the Great Northern Diver in Britain. They succeed in saving the eggs from the clutches of a villainous egg thief. The author makes much play of mystifying the location but it seems to be the Tolsta coast of Lewis. The novel's narrative strength lies in the skill with which processes such as sailing in fog or bird-watching are handled. In Ransome's characteristic make-believe the five girls assume Little Women roles, Dick is seen as the Ship's Naturalist and their uncle the skipper is Captain Flint. One curious aspect of the fantasy is that Lewis locals are represented as Punch-type caricatures: the Laird and his son are be-tartaned 'chieftains', the M'Gintys, and their estate workers are 'savage Gaels' who speak no English. Nowadays young readers are likely to find much to argue about in this forgotten classic.

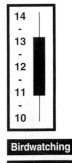

Birdwatching

Conservation

Hebrides

Nature

Sailing

GREYFRIARS BOBBY
Eleanor Atkinson
Harper, 1912 (op); Puffin Classics, 1994, ISBN:014036742X

Drawing on historical fact and Edinburgh myth this American novel explores one of the commonest themes of animal fiction, the bond between dogs and human beings. It tells of how Bobby, a terrier, stubbornly refuses to desert his master's grave. A strength is the attractive presentation of the behaviour of one particular breed, the Skye Terrier, an animal noted for its loyalty, courage and agility. Although other creatures such as the birds in the Greyfriars churchyard are treated anthropomorphically, Bobby is honestly observed. One dramatic episode is the terrier's near-fatal descent over the Castle Rock in an encroaching haar. The setting is a highly coloured, melodramatic picture of the squalor of the Grassmarket of Edinburgh in the 1860s. Despite kailyairdy couthiness, characters such as the caretaker, the innkeeper and the Lord Provost are convincingly presented. The narrative seems flawed today by its sentimental moralising but it has been immensely popular and is worth offering to older, persistent readers interested in animals. A Disney film version appeared in 1961 and the material has been reworked recently for younger readers by Lavinia Derwent and by Ruth Brown.

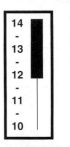

Dogs

Loyalty

Edinburgh

Poverty

14
-
13
-
12
-
11
-
10

Adventure

History

Jacobites

North America

Wolves

THE LAST WOLF
Michael Morpurgo
Doubleday, 2002; Corgi, 2003, ISBN:0440865077

This short, beautifully illustrated tale for younger readers combines themes of Jacobite exile after the Forty-Five and the bonding of humans and animals. During a spell of convalescence the narrator has been bullied by his granddaughter to research their family history by computer. He discovers a distant relative in Boston who sends him an account written in old age by an ancestor, Robbie MacLeod, telling how he came to flee to North America after Culloden. The fanciful story, which seems custom-built for a Disney film, tells how Redcoats kill what they consider the last wolf in Scotland. One of her cubs escapes, however, and is rescued by young Robbie. Named Charlie in honour of the Bonnie Prince, the cub is smuggled across the Atlantic by Robbie and he helps him set up home in the forest wilderness of Vermont. Eventually Charlie succumbs to the call of the wild and is last seen with his own brood of cubs. The aged Robbie's reminiscences are in slightly ornate English which give the central narrative a period flavour. This unusual, highly sentimental book is likely to provoke differing reactions among readers.

14
-
13
-
12
-
11
-
10

Cats

Fantasy

History

Humour

Orkney

Storytelling

SIX LIVES OF FANKLE THE CAT
George Mackay Brown
Chatto & Windus, 1980 (op); Floris Kelpies, 2002, ISBN:0863154034

Jenny is an imaginative girl who lives in an Orkney village. When her only friend old Sanders goes away, she adopts a little black cat, Fankle, who can talk when he chooses. His tales reveal that he has already consumed several of his nine lives in colourful encounters across the centuries. He spends a year with Jenny until a speeding van consumes his fifth life. Much later Jenny, now an old woman, creates for her grandchildren a tale of how Fankle in yet another life saves the world from hostile moon creatures.

The theme of the book is the power of narrative. Living as she does for story making, Jenny projects her skill on to Fankle. The village schoolchildren are asked to write about Fankle, and their efforts make up the central chapter of the novel. There is stimulus here for readers' own writing. Mackay Brown modulates the mood delicately – amusing, roistering and touching. Underlying there is a wistful reminder that all lives, not only Fankle's, are brief and that humans, unlike cats, have only one.

STRING LUG THE FOX
David Stephen

Lutterworth Press, 1950 (op); Century, 1985, ISBN:0712608826 (op)

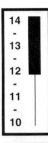

The scene is the farmlands of north Lanarkshire at the beginning of the Second World War. Through this landscape prowls a fox surviving resourcefully in a hostile world. The cast include his vixens, other animals and the country folk who are his adversaries. One of these, Jock Simpson the fencer, reluctantly respects the fox. The story traces String Lug's life over three years. His nature is to kill and he spends much of his time doing that. Among key episodes are birth, mating, combat and violent death. Other incidents include the horrors of moorland fire, ambushes and night raids on hen runs. String Lug's enemies do not ride to hounds: they prefer shotguns, traps, poisons and terriers. Main themes are the relationship of humans and animals, and the impact of man on the natural world. The narrative movingly evokes the passing seasons. The fox has his own personality but is not sentimentalised and the humans are ambivalent towards his depredations. The novel presupposes interest in animals but its vigorous pace will appeal to many young readers.

Foxes

Life cycle

Nature

Violence

FAMILY

14
13
12
11
10

Adventure

Growing up

Highlands

THE BATTLE OF WEDNESDAY WEEK
Barbara Willard
Constable, 1963 (op); Puffin, 1976, ISBN:0140303596 (op)

This novel starts in the south of England and Massachusetts but its main location is a remote township on a West Highland sea loch. Occurring over one summer in the early sixties, it involves two middle-class, single-parent families, one American and one English. When the English mother and the American father, who have both been widowed, decide to marry, they are faced with the challenge of integrating their broods of wary children. Their strategy is the enforced intimacy of a holiday in a beloved cottage by the lochside. The plot hinges on clashes of character and culture among the six step-children, ranging in age between 9 and 16. Its strength lies in the differing personalities of the youngsters, as they get to know one another through various ploys and scrapes. In some ways the novel may now seem innocently old-fashioned: today's readers may for example find the supporting cast of good-natured local Gaels less than convincing. Nonetheless the story is skilfully handled and is still likely to hold interest and stimulate discussion among younger readers.

14
13
12
11
10

Change

Island life

Love

Outsiders

EMMA'S ISLAND
Honor Arundel
Hamish Hamilton, 1968 (op); Pan, 1972, ISBN:0330232185 (op)

The *Emma* trilogy follows the many changes in the life of the eponymous heroine after the tragic death of her parents. Firstly she lives in Edinburgh with her artistic Aunt Patsy in *The High House*; secondly moves to a new home on an island off the west coast of Scotland with Aunt Patsy and Uncle Stephen in *Emma's Island*, and thirdly returns to Edinburgh for her final school year in *Emma in Love*. In this book, the second part of the trilogy, Emma has to adjust to the many practical problems of living on a remote island. She has to help her aunt and uncle set up a new home and run an art gallery. The arrival of her baby cousin Vanessa brings emotional and practical difficulties which she manages to overcome. Coping with school examinations also makes demands on her time. She enjoys the excitement of a first foreign holiday with her brother Richard and friends, when she discovers that she is not as plain and uninteresting as she thought. Finally on an archaeological dig she meets Alastair, a University student from Glasgow, with whom she experiences the joys of first love.

THE HOUSE ON THE HILL
Eileen Dunlop
Canongate, 1989 (op); Floris Kelpies, 2000, ISBN:0862412447

14
-
13
-
12
-
11
-
10

Susan Gilmore and Philip North find themselves living with their spinster Aunt Jane in a huge, old-fashioned and uncomfortable house in the west end of Glasgow. Philip is initially resentful of his mother's 'dumping' him on Aunt Jane while she trains to be a nurse following his father's death, and makes no effort to be pleasant. It is the discovery of a mysterious light in an empty room, and the determination to find out what is going on which brings the cousins together. Although the room looks empty, ghostly outlines of the furniture which used to be there can be picked up on photographs, and gradually the original life of the room returns, bringing with it both fear and the possibility of solving an even greater mystery: what happened to Jane's fiancé who left her for the Front in 1914 promising to send an engagement ring back to her?

Themes of family feuds, peer pressure at school, courage and weakness, in addition to the essential solving of the mystery, make this novel a page-turner. The characters are finely drawn and lifelike, and the contrasts between the enclosed atmosphere of the house on the hill and the outside world enhance the special relationships which are built up.

Glasgow
History
Love
Mystery
Supernatural

KEZZIE
Theresa Breslin
Mammoth, 1994 (op); Egmont, 2002, ISBN:140520110X

14
-
13
-
12
-
11
-
10

This novel could easily have degenerated into melodrama, but Breslin maintains a sense of realism in her vivid depiction of the difficulties facing Kezzie Munro after her father is killed in a mine disaster. The first section sees Kezzie's family suffering the trials of the Depression of the late 1930s, the grandfather reduced to begging in the streets until Kezzie bluffs her way into a factory job. No sooner have matters improved than, as a result of another accident, Kezzie's younger sister Lucy is picked up as a wandering child and transported to Canada for adoption. In the second part of the novel, Kezzie follows her to Canada, travelling coast to coast before she finds her, traumatised and barely responsive. Breslin takes the opportunity to describe the glories of the Canadian landscape, moderating by so doing the potential pathos of the plot.

Finally, as expected, both girls will return to Scotland, their prospects greatly improved. It is to Breslin's credit that this does not read as a contrived 'happy ever after' ending.

Canada
Emigration
Growing up
History

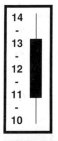

14
-
13
-
12
-
11
-
10

Divorce

Humour

MADAME DOUBTFIRE
Anne Fine
Hamish Hamilton, 1987 (op); Puffin, 1995, ISBN:0140373551

For some young readers this moving novel will strike home very directly. It is a sharply funny and painful account of the effects of a divorce upon the three children of the marriage. The 'exes' are a hopelessly incompatible pair: Miranda is a brittle, tempestuous redhead intent upon her career; and Daniel is an anarchic, slobbish, out-of-work actor with a clown's sense of humour and ample capacity for self-pity. The miseries of their three children, caught in divided loyalties, express themselves variously in tension, confusion, resignation and fury. Lydia, the eldest, reveals a knowingness worthy of a member of Miss Brodie's gang. The narrative hinges on a masquerade in outrageous drag which enables Daniel to maintain regular access to Miranda and the children, posing as Madame Doubtfire, a perfect treasure of a housekeeper. The ploy climaxes and collapses when Daniel's other job as a nude model in a life-class at Art College intrudes farcically, and all is revealed. The ensuing rage and nastiness of the adults abate only when the three children speak out for their own rights. No lasting reconciliation seems likely, but thanks to a hapless pet quail the novel closes on a lyric note of momentary happiness.

14
-
13
-
12
-
11
-
10

Mystery

Quest

Refugees

Russian Revolution

NATASHA'S WILL
Joan Lingard
Puffin, 2000; New Century Readers, 2003, ISBN:0582488540

This ingenious novel starts with a title which proves to be a pun. The structure is complex, involving parallel quests in two different eras and places; and it develops via a paper chase of riddles scattered through a library of children's books. However the style is attractively simple and direct, suiting a younger readership than the author's Maggie and Kevin and Sadie series.

One storyline shows Natasha, an aristocratic Russian girl, escaping with her family from the horrors of the Bolshevik revolution. The alternating narrative set in present-day Scotland concerns a family desperately searching for the will of their late Russian benefactress which may save them being evicted from the home she had informally shared with them in the West Highlands. The link between the two stories is that the emigré Natasha had married a Scotsman, and came to live out her long happy life in the old house by the loch. Before she died she had devised for her young Scottish friends and carers a riddling challenge to find her hidden will. Things go disastrously wrong when a distant Russian descendant of Natasha turns up claiming that the estate is legally his. As in all such tantalising tales, there is a just-in-time happy ending.

SECOND CHANCE
Alison Prince
Barrington Stoke, 2000, ISBN:1902260465

This small gem of a novel is likely to prove an arresting read for most younger teenagers. It is an affectionate, unjudgmental account of a family who might easily figure in the media as 'the neighbours from hell'. It is also a ghost story. Structure and style are accessible to less confident readers and are supported by the author's own illustrations. Ross the narrator is 15. His mother Cathy, who already has 8 children, is pregnant again. Steve her amiable partner is unemployed but kennels greyhounds in their council house in the hope that one day he will make his fortune at the dog track. When the Council expels the family in response to neighbours' complaints, they squat in a derelict wooden cafe on the beach. The mood darkens when Ross encounters Zac, a spectral boy of his own age who was driven to suicide by the heartlessness of his father, a previous owner of the cafe. This lonely spirit is laid to rest and in a sense gets a second chance through the birth of Cathy's ninth child, who is to be called Zachary.

14 - 13 - 12 - 11 - 10

Eviction

Ghosts

Homelessness

Outsiders

THE SHERWOOD HERO
Alison Prince
Macmillan, 2002, ISBN:0330400282

This is clever storytelling. Young Kelly reports what happens when she starts to work recent painful events into a story for her school's English project. Her task is prompted by a visiting author and her personal model is the folktale of Robin Hood. Kelly's project narrative threads its way in italics through the book. Set in 1990s Glasgow the novel tackles a moral dilemma: it explores the idea that economically 'it's every man for himself'. Kelly's socialist grandfather challenges this view and inadvertently gives her the idea that theft can sometimes be justified. In a moment of folly she steals a credit card and experiences the frightening realities of 'robbing the rich to give to the poor'. Fictionalizing the episode reawakens Kelly's guilt and precipitates a new crisis of family trust. The writing is strong in contrasts: between Kelly's former life in London and her new life in a Glasgow tenement; between Kelly's family and that of her Indian friend Angie. An obvious temptation is to use this novel as a stimulus for writing. Above all it is an ingenious and thought-provoking story for older readers.

14 - 13 - 12 - 11 - 10

Crime

Glasgow

School

Storytelling

SO FAR FROM SKYE
Judith O'Neill
Hamish Hamilton, 1992 (op); Puffin, 1993, ISBN:0140349804

Dedicated to the memory of the authors' own great-great grandparents who were forced to emigrate from Skye to Australia during the famine clearances of 1852, this novel tells the story of two fictitious children, Morag and Allan MacDonald, their family and their entire community who leave their homes forever. They travel with many other families from Skye to Greenock, then on to Victoria in Australia. Surviving the hardships and perils of an epic journey by sea and land, they learn a new way of life on the other side of the world, ironically working on a sheep farm in the outback. They have to adapt quickly in what seems like another planet, but they still carry much of their native culture and its values, which is why they can sympathise so much with the aborigines who have also been dispossessed. There is a fascinating, vivid description of the journey and a well-paced narrative with interesting characters and relationships. This novel really brings the past to life and is a great celebration of human courage and resilience.

Australia

Clearances

Emigration

Skye

SO FAR TO GO
Rhodri Jones
Andre Deutsch Ltd, 1987 (op); Canongate Kelpies, 1989, ISBN:0862412498 (op)

When Ian's Dad finds a new job in London the whole family leave Glasgow in search of a better life down south, but things soon start to go wrong when his sister Bella and brother Jimmy can't find jobs and the feckless Jimmy soon lands in trouble with the police. Before long they are wishing they were back in Glasgow, especially when their father's job comes under threat. Unable to find any friends of his own age, Ian lands in a fight on his first day at school with gang leader Vincent, a black boy who ridicules Ian's accent and later taunts him about his sister Bella being 'on the game'. Ironically this incident leads to an unexpected friendship with his former enemy Vincent and a gradual change in fortune for Ian.

There is a gripping storyline with realistic characters and relevant themes of teenagers coping with change, relationships and prejudice.

Friendship

Prejudice

School

Unemployment

THE SPUDDY
Lillian Beckwith

Hutchison, 1974 (op); Chivers, 1999, ISBN:0754036243 (op)

Set in a fictitious west coast fishing town this is the story of the Spuddy, a scruffy mongrel, who finds himself abandoned by his dead master's widow, just as Andy, a dumb eight year old, arrives in town, having been abandoned by his mother in Glasgow. Though well looked after by his aunt and uncle, Andy is unable to make any friends of his own age, but he soon finds a soul mate in the Spuddy. Together they spend most of the day watching the fishing boats, especially *The Silver Crest*, skippered by Jake, another lonely figure whose wife has left with their young son. When Jake forms a friendship with the dumb boy, a new home is found for the dog and a deep friendship and loyalty develops among all three. The novel tackles themes of friendship, loyalty and responsibility. It has a simple storyline, good descriptions and atmosphere, but difficult language in places.

14
-
13
-
12
-
11
-
10

Disability

Dogs

Fishing

Friendship

Loyalty

GROWING UP

14
-
13
-
12
-
11
-
10

Disability

Friendship

Heroism

Old age

World War II

BUNGEE HERO
Julie Bertagna
Barrington Stoke, 1999, ISBN:1902260910

This thought-provoking, unsentimental tale is accessible to less confident readers. At first sight neither of its main characters is particularly lovable. Adam is a football-daft teenager and Mr Haddock is an embittered limbless resident in the local old folk's home. Adam's mother cajoles him into taking Haddock out in his wheelchair. He resents the chore and when he meets the old man they interact boorishly. Things go from bad to worse, but in the end the two discover dramatically that they have much in common.

The plot hinges on the neat use of a story within a story. Adam gets the chance to read Haddock's wartime diary of his exploits as a parachutist on a mission over occupied France. Having just experienced the fear and fascination of heights on a white-knuckle fairground ride, the boy sees behind Haddock's cantankerous facade, and decides to exorcise his own terror by tackling a sponsored bungee jump on the old man's behalf. The narrative climaxes on the huge dockyard crane by the city's riverside. Its spectacular ending leaves readers metaphorically to jump to their own conclusion.

14
-
13
-
12
-
11
-
10

Class

Clearances

Highlands

Love

Old age

THE CLEARANCE
Joan Lingard
Hamish Hamilton 1973 (op); Macmillan, 1994, ISBN:0330332899 (op)

A summer holiday in the Highlands proves a turning point for a maturing adolescent. Maggie is a headstrong, intelligent girl who comes grudgingly from the city to help her grandmother living in a remote Inverness-shire cottage in the 1960s. The narrative confronts the predicament of a very old person in failing health who toughly clings to her independence. What can possibly be done for her? It also contrasts the cultures of an easygoing working-class Glasgow family and their aspiring middle-class Edinburgh counterpart. The developing summer romance between Maggie and her new Edinburgh friend James is reticently sketched. 'Clearance' is shown to have three meanings: firstly the Greenyards evictions which drove Maggie's ancestors out of Easter Ross in 1845; then the accidental fire which forces her Granny into sheltered accommodation in a nearby town; and latterly the municipal housing policy which may decant Maggie and her own immediate family from their Glasgow tenement to a high rise flat in the outskirts of the city. The mood is skilfully varied and there is much for reflection and discussion.

THE DEATH OR GLORY BOYS
Theresa Breslin
Methuen 1996 (op); Egmont Books, 2002, ISBN:1405201096

Sarah, Phil, Maggie and David are four teenagers out shopping for boots for Sarah, joking and teasing each other in a normal way, when they are affected by the impact of a bomb set off by a lone terrorist. Gradually they are not only drawn into the age-old arguments about the need to fight versus the need to keep the peace, but also learn these through personal experience when first Sarah and then the others take part in an army careers exercise. The influence of the war poets read at school, their own hopes for the future, the need to take life and death decisions in the war games and how to resolve the conflicts of all these influences are the themes of the book. All the while in the background a terrorist is about to catch up with them. This is a convincing and very readable novel which addresses major issues in an intelligent way without being boring. The language and style are clear, modern and straightforward.

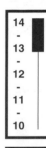

14
13
12
11
10

Adventure

Northern Ireland

Outsiders

EMMA IN LOVE
Honor Arundel
Hamish Hamilton, 1970 (op); Pan, 1995, ISBN:0330234692 (op)

At the end of the summer, 18-year-old Emma returns to Edinburgh to sit her Highers and share a small flat with her brother Richard. Although money is short and she has to do most of the housework, her boyfriend Alastair is only 50 miles away in Glasgow. She eagerly awaits his phone calls, letters and occasional meetings, but as winter sets in Emma discovers that love can also be cruel. She increasingly feels that Alastair's feelings have cooled, especially when he prefers to go skiing at Christmas with friends instead of returning to their island home with her.

The themes are growing up, relationships, and love. The first person narrative voice sounds a bit too adult at times, but the story of a sensitive teenager coping with change has a strong appeal, especially for girls.

Edinburgh

Friendship

Love

School

14
13
12
11
10

Farming

History

North-east

Old age

FARMER'S BOY
John R. Allan
Methuen, 1935 (op); Mercat Press, 1999, ISBN:1873644868

This novel, with elements of autobiography and documentary, is in the category of memories of traditional Scottish farming life, making its first appearance only three years after Gibbon's *Sunset Song*. It deals with a boy's early years growing up on his grandfather's farm in Aberdeenshire before and during the First World War, and describes the way of life on the farm, the people and the places, vividly and sympathetically. Whereas Gibbon in *Sunset Song* highlights the bleak and negative aspects of rural life, Allan is always positive and frequently amusing. Yet he is not sentimental and presents the reader with a keenly observed account of a changing society. The picture of the grandfather, the 'Old Man of Dungair', is a classic portrayal of a strong local character, whose death marks the end of an era. The style of the book may be rather difficult for average readers, but repays the effort of reading; there are, however, many episodes within the story worth looking at on their own.

14
13
12
11
10

Bullying

Conservation

Family

Hebrides

Nature

FINN'S ISLAND
Eileen Dunlop
Blackie, 1991 (op); Puffin, 1994, ISBN:0140369066 (op)

Although the past is a strong theme in this novel, Finn Lochlan, the main character, never actually finds himself in the past, as Dunlop's other protagonists frequently do. Finn is fascinated by his late grandfather's tales of life on Hirsay, the outermost of the Outer Hebrides, an island abandoned by its population sixty years previously. Finn's dream of returning to the island is fulfilled in a way that he had not expected, when he accompanies agricultural student Douglas Cooper and his family to search for a rare plant, known to grow only there. A series of misadventures turn the expedition into a nightmare, but Finn is finally able to understand what life on the island must really have been like and to put his grandfather's stories into perspective.

There are several competing themes in this fascinating narrative. Father-son relationships, bullying at school, learning difficulties, ecological and environmental concerns, the importance of wild places and their protection and the importance of keeping dreams separate from real life are all illustrated through the interactions of the small number of perfectly-drawn characters. Competent younger readers would derive a good deal of pleasure and food for thought from this novel.

THE FREEDOM MACHINE
Joan Lingard
Hamish Hamilton, 1986 (op); Puffin, 1988, ISBN:0140323694 (op)

Jim has to go to stay with relatives in Fife because his mother is ill, but he over-hears something being said which gives him the impression that he is not wanted. He decides to take off on his bike, Gulliver, and find a new life for himself, until his mother is better enough to have him back again. This is a children's picaresque novel: Jim encounters various types of humanity on his journey, finally ending up with the rather clichéd and idealised grandfather who puts everything right with his aunt and basically saves the day.

Children relate well to the novel, as it speaks to them in their own language, and there are many thought-provoking ideas and themes to explore.

14
13
12
11
10

Family

Fife

Quest

ON THE ISLAND
Iain Crichton Smith
Gollancz, 1979 (op); Richard Drew, 1998, ISBN:0862672260 (op)

This is clearly drawn from the author's own upbringing and is a series of episodes in the life of young Iain, his mother, his brother Kenneth and their neighbours before and during the Second World War. The book's short chapters build up into a picture of a community with its poverty, its pride, and its relationship with the outside world as seen through the eyes of Iain. It is a realistic picture, unflinching not only in its acknowledgement of adult failings and childhood jealousies but also in its portrayal of Iain's mother, a hard and proud woman, hurting in her poverty and seeing in her clever son a means of turning the tables on a critical world. There are many touching moments such as when Iain discovers the joys of adventure stories or the special feeling of being alone in a wild place. This is a multi-layered book and older readers will note such points as the ironies of the irrelevance of the classical curriculum to the reality of life and the reactions of the adults to the cruelties of war, but younger readers will surely recognise the genuineness of childhood recollections and appreciate the special flavour of its time and place.

14
13
12
11
10

Hebrides

History

Island life

Outsiders

Poverty

14
-
13
-
12
-
11
-
10

Class

Family

Glasgow

Love

THE RESETTLING
Joan Lingard
Hamish Hamilton, 1975 (op); Red Fox, 1995, ISBN:060020300X (op)

The setting is Glasgow in the late 1960s, with occasional forays to Edinburgh. Maggie Graham is trying to study for her Higher Grade examinations but faces serious distractions. Her family have been 'resettled' from their tenement home to the 11th floor of a new tower block. Somehow or other Maggie has to come to the aid of her mother who is so depressed by this displacement that she is on sedation. A related challenge is that she needs to inject some drive into her father's flagging plumber's business which she helped to set up. Above all she is trying to cope with her growing relationship with James, a privately educated Edinburgh boy living comfortably in the bourgeois splendours of Heriot Row. Without stereotyping, the story touches perceptively on the differing social assumptions of Edinburgh and Glasgow. What constitute proper ambitions for a very able girl? *The Resettling* can stand alone as a thought-provoking read, but it gains if taken as sequel to Maggie's Highland venture in *The Clearance*. Maggie's progress continues in the *The Pilgrimage* and *The Reunion*.

14
-
13
-
12
-
11
-
10

Fife

Friendship

Humour

Nature

ROBBIE
Emil Pacholek
Andre Deutsch, 1980 (op); Floris Kelpies 1995, ISBN:0862411130

Set in the small Fife village of Kincapel in the 1950s, this is a memorable celebration of a boy growing up in a close knit rural community at a time when traditional ways are giving way to the modern world, with the arrival of television, jet aeroplanes zooming overhead, tractors replacing horses in the fields and trees being cut down around the village. Love and appreciation of the old ways are passed on to Robbie, especially through his grandfather's wit and wisdom. The boy therefore discovers the mysteries of the natural world and enjoys the customs and celebrations of the changing seasons. He learns to cope with bullies and laugh at the funny aspects of life. He must come to terms with sorrow and death, but also enjoys several mischievous and exciting adventures with a wild tinker boy McPhee who becomes his best friend. This beautifully written classic of Scottish childhood is funny, fascinating, moving, exciting and timeless.

A SOUND OF CHARIOTS
Mollie Hunter
Hamish Hamilton, 1973 (op); HarperCollins, 1994, ISBN:0064402355 (op)

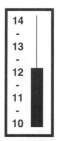

14
-
13
-
12
-
11
-
10

This is certainly the finest novel about growing up in Scotland available for older readers in the 12–14 range. It is a portrait of the artist as a young girl, a challenging but rich exploration of the personality of Bridie McShane. She is an intense, stubbornly talented child living in rural Longniddry on the Firth of Forth after World War I. When her Irish father, a disabled veteran and an independent-minded Marxist, dies young, her deeply religious mother is left to rear her large family in poverty. Bridie loves story-telling and poetry. She is haunted by the untimely loss of her father whom she worships, and by her own developing power with language, 'the gift of the gab', according to her mother. The mysteries of death and time are enshrined for Bridie in precious lines by Andrew Marvel:

> 'But at my back I always hear
> Time's winged chariot hurrying near.'

The novel takes her from the age of 8 until she leaves school at 14 to work in Edinburgh, determined against the odds to make her father live on through her writing.

Family

Forth valley

Poverty

Storytelling

THE TRUST
Alan Hermus
Scottish Children's Press, 1998, ISBN:1899827641

14
-
13
-
12
-
11
-
10

Ranald MacPhee, a wandering tinker boy, lives by the old way of life on the road, learning the traditional skills and wisdom of his ancestors from his grandfather, Old Hector, who claims to be descended from a seal wife. When the old man dies, Ranald is visited by the old man in a dream and charged with the sacred trust of carrying out his grandfather's last wish which leads him on a quest. With his old pony Dochas as his only companion he battles against the odds, evading the clutches of the law and the Social and facing the hazards of crossing a mountain pass in winter in order to reach his goal. Yet his grandfather's voice is still there to guide and protect him, telling him 'to be true to himself' as he fights to keep his promise, and find new meaning in his own life in a changing modern world.

This is a moving story of loyalty, determination, survival, compassion and love for a way of life fast disappearing. It has a central character and themes most children will warm to.

Celtic tradition

Loyalty

Quest

Supernatural

Travelling folk

HISTORY

14
-
13
-
12
-
11
-
10

Boxing

Class

Disability

Fife

THE BAILLIE'S DAUGHTER
Donald Lightwood
Canongate Kelpies, 1990, ISBN:0862412854 (op)

Set within reach of the golf links in pious, prosperous St Andrews in 1852, this episodic tale displays bold characterisation and dialogue. In a historical context it challenges young readers with issues of handicap, respectability, class and religion. There are ample opportunities for discussion and dramatic activities. Janet, a 14-year-old orphan girl, has to make her own way in the world. She gains a position in the well-to-do household of Baillie Douglas, looking after the only child Jeanie, a Down's Syndrome girl of her own age, who is locked away from sight upstairs. Starting off as the 'Daftie's' warder, Janet, through her spontaneous affection, demonstrates that Jeanie is more able to learn and develop than her parents believe. For reasons that gradually emerge they have chosen to regard her condition as punishment visited upon them by God. Caught up in Janet's fortunes is the English atheist Cope, a travelling bare-knuckle fighter. The fast-moving narrative plunges the doomed Douglas family into Ibsenesque depths before surfacing in a hint of happiness for the resilient Janet and Cope as they finally put St Andrews behind them.

14
-
13
-
12
-
11
-
10

Covenanters

Jacobites

Love

War

BONNIE DUNDEE
Rosemary Sutcliff
Bodley Head (op), 1983; Red Fox, 1994, ISBN:009935411X

Hugh Herriott, from an Ayrshire family of Covenanters, tells the story of how as a young man he came to follow the fortunes of the Royalist soldier John Graham of Claverhouse, who later became the Jacobite leader Viscount Dundee. The story covers the suppression of the Covenanters and the Jacobite rising after the coming of William of Orange up to and after the battle of Killiecrankie. The Scottish atmosphere and tone are well handled and the later seventeenth-century history is made clear and interesting, although Claverhouse may be presented in too ideal and flattering a light. The story includes both strong action and a love interest for young readers of both sexes.

BONNIE PRINCE CHARLIE: A TALE OF FONTENOY AND CULLODEN

G.A. Henty

Blackie, 1887 (op); Preston-Speed, 2000, IBSN:188715955X

Published shortly after Stevenson's *Kidnapped*, this novel reveals an early use of Scottish history as fiction for young readers. Ronald Leslie, teenage son of an exiled Jacobite, is the protégé of a mercenary soldier, Malcolm Anderson, who aids his escape from Glasgow to the Continent in 1740. The two adventurers enlist in the Scottish Dragoons in French service. After distinguishing himself at the battle of Fontenoy and reuniting his imprisoned parents, Ronald returns to Scotland with Charles Edward Stuart in 1745 and fights through the Jacobite campaign to its sorry end. Henty skilfully varies the focus of his narrative. He can zoom in vividly on one fictional episode then pull back to a wide-angled take on historical events. His handling of the friendship of Ronald and his older companion is convincing, though lacking the subtleties of Stevenson's pairing of David Balfour and Alan Breck. Henty briskly preaches to his 'dear lads' (for he assumes that all his readers are boys) that it was good for the future of Britain that Charles Edward failed, but the ensuing story does dramatise the ambivalent loyalties of the '45. Older, confident readers might explore this neglected but surprisingly competent adventure yarn in conjunction with *Kidnapped*.

14
13
12
11
10

Adventure

Family

Jacobites

War

THE BURNING HILL

Iona McGregor

Faber & Faber, 1970, ISBN:0571093183 (op)

This is an unsentimental love story for thoughtful readers in the 12–14 range. It is set in Fife during Scotland's economic take-off in the 1770s. Gauchely at first, affection grows between Jean, daughter of an impoverished laird, and Robin, son of a nouveau riche neighbour. Both are at odds with parental authority. She resents being brought back from Edinburgh to a dull life on a country estate. He wants a career with the new technologies of the Carron iron works, and rebels against his father's determination to get him an army commission. In hopes of exploiting his property, Jean's father has miners excavate old coal workings in search of ironstone. Sabotage however reignites subterranean fires which destroy his neighbour's new plantings. The friendship of the parents turns sour; Jean and Robin marry clandestinely, and a duel brings the death of one laird and the exiling of the other. Bankruptcy and entail swiftly ruin both families but the young couple, with a child in the offing, bravely face their future in a new industrial Scotland. Niceties of class and the status of the womenfolk are tellingly presented in this novel.

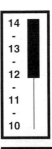

14
13
12
11
10

Class

Fife

Love

Mining

14
13
12
11
10

Clans

Jacobites

Love

Loyalty

THE DARK MILE
D.K. Broster
Heinemann, 1929 (op); in THE JACOBITE TRILOGY, Lomond Books, 1994, ISBN:1842040324

Set ten years after the events, the final part of Broster's Jacobite trilogy deals with the fate of the defeated Highland clans who had supported the Stuart cause in 1745. The focus shifts from Ewan Cameron to his cousin, Ian Stewart of Invernacree, who falls in love with Olivia Campbell, and to the bitterness of their two clans. This is a more overt love story than the previous novels and perhaps too romantic for some young readers. But the themes of loyalty and betrayal are continued as Ewan, despite his promise never to seek revenge, searches for the person who betrayed Archie Cameron. The narrative is swift and engaging, the plot well-constructed, and the settings in location and time are convincing. The characterisation of heroes and villains offers identifiable figures to whom the reader can relate. The other two novels in the trilogy are *The Flight of the Heron* and *The Gleam in the North*.

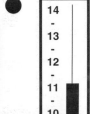

14
13
12
11
10

Adventure

Edinburgh

Fife

Loyalty

The Reformation

THE DARK SHADOW
Mary Rhind
Canongate, 1988 (op); Floris Kelpies, 2002, ISBN:0863154069

The year is 1560 and the Reformation in Scotland has taken a powerful hold. The story opens in Crail. Davie lives there with his mother, stepfather and his blind little sister Lizzie. Davie wants to make a pilgrimage with her to the Well of St Triduana in Restalrig, where he believes the waters will restore her eyesight. Their uncle Father Andrew arranges a boat to take them to the Lothian shore and they make for Restalrig, pursued all the way by the shadowy figure of a 'leper' dressed in black. The waters have no effect, so they proceed to Edinburgh where they find relatives who look after them. On hearing that the Reformers are burning down the Church at Restalrig they return to attempt to rescue two priests who had been kind to them. Amid the rioting Lizzie is thrown down a stair. In her fall her sight is restored. She is taken to safety by the 'leper' and the story draws to a happy conclusion.

The characterisation is straightforward and easily accessible to young readers. Period details are well drawn and the Reformation is sensitively handled, showing there were people of good will on both sides.

THE EAGLE OF THE NINTH
Rosemary Sutcliff
Oxford, 1954 (op); Oxford University Press, 2000, ISBN:0192750453

Marcus Flavius Aquila, a young centurion in the Roman Second Legion serving in Britain, is wounded and made unfit for further military service. Bored with civilian life, he turns his attention to finding out the truth about the disappearance of his father and the Ninth Legion in the north of Britain some years before. Accompanied by his faithful friend and former slave Esca, Marcus goes on a secret mission north of Hadrian's Wall to find the truth and if possible to bring back the Eagle standard of his father's lost legion. The trail leads them to the west of Caledonia, where their quest is accomplished. The action is well described and the Roman and Celtic atmospheres are interestingly brought to life. This novel is the first in a sequence about the Aquila family in Roman Britain. The series culminates in *Frontier Wolf.*

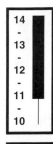

14
-
13
-
12
-
11
-
10

Adventure

Mystery

Romans

West Scotland

AN EDINBURGH REEL
Iona McGregor
Faber & Faber, 1968 (op); Canongate Kelpies, 1986, ISBN:0862411327 (op)

This novel is set in Edinburgh in the years after the '45 in the household of John Murray, a returned Jacobite attempting to restart his life, claim back his possessions and find and punish the man who betrayed him. It is told from the viewpoint of his teenage daughter, Christine, and there is a fine mix of characters through whom Iona McGregor brings the period to life: tradespeople, soldiers, children, servants and aristocrats. John Murray discovers what happened in his past but also learns that his and others' future lies in the new ways of trade and scientific improvement, a process of learning in which his daughter participates as she also pursues her own romantic interests. The novel conveys the tension and violence of the times and there is plenty of excitement with the city guard, cockfights and swordplay but it also deals with the way the old medieval attitudes had to change to create modern Scotland. This is one of the most significant Scottish historical novels written for children. It has a lively, readable style.

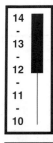

14
-
13
-
12
-
11
-
10

Adventure

Edinburgh

Jacobites

Love

14
-
13
-
12
-
11
-
10

Adventure

Fife

Growing up

Love

Mary Q. of Scots

ESCAPE FROM LOCH LEVEN
Mollie Hunter
Canongate, 1987 (op); Floris Kelpies, 2003, ISBN:086315414X

This novel is, among other things, a painless way of learning a good deal of Scottish history. Will Douglas, the bastard son of Sir William Douglas, Keeper of Loch Leven Castle, becomes central to the plot to free Mary Queen of Scots when she is imprisoned in the castle and forced to abdicate in favour of her infant son.

Will is not your common or garden boy hero. He is resourceful and intelligent, and it is purely through bad luck that his own plan to free the queen does not succeed. However, he has some serious character flaws to overcome before he can again become a trusted intimate of the queen. He does become infatuated with Mary as a woman, and puts his own life in danger several times to bring her comfort.

The background is historically accurate, and gives an excellent sense of the political intrigues which surround the queen at this time. The characterisation is vivid and fully realised. Will's first person narrative is used as a means of conveying the complexity of the character to the more mature reader.

14
-
13
-
12
-
11
-
10

Adventure

Fife

Witch-hunts

ESCAPE IN DARKNESS
Kathleen Fidler
Lutterworth Press, 1961 (op); Canongate Kelpies, 1987, ISBN: 0862411572 (op)

The murky politics of early 17th century Scotland form the background to this dramatic novel. James Bruce, with his great aunt Barbara Ruthven, travels from exile in Holland to Culross to bury his father's heart and claim his right to his father's lands. Made welcome by Sir George Bruce, they settle in the town and in due course James buries the heart in the abbey. Barbara Ruthven's skill with herbal medicines earns the trust of the coal miners' children but arouses jealousy and suspicion in the community. Immobilised by a stroke, Sir George Bruce is no longer able to protect her and she is accused of witchcraft and imprisoned in the abbey tower. She is rescued by the joint endeavours of James, the Bruce grandchildren and a tinker girl who works in the mine, and escapes with James to Holland. James rejects his claim to his inheritance and chooses instead to study medicine in Leiden.

The well-paced narrative culminates in a sequence of dramatic scenes: the great storm, the flooding of the mine, the witch-hunt and the daring escape from the tower. Culross, with its saltpans, trading ships and undersea coalmine is skilfully brought to life and the atmosphere of political intrigue and superstition is powerfully evoked.

THE FLIGHT OF THE HERON
D.K. Broster

Heinemann, 1925 (op); in THE JACOBITE TRILOGY, Lomond Books, 1994, ISBN:1842040324

Set mainly in the West Highlands immediately before, during and after the Jacobite Rebellion of 1745, this is a romantic adventure story following the fortunes of Ewan Cameron, a cadet laird of that clan, who is wholeheartedly devoted to his chief. His fate turns out to be intertwined with that of Captain Keith Windham, a dedicated Hanoverian officer whom he captures at the initial confrontation at Spean Bridge. Events move quickly through the Rebellion and the three meetings of the central characters, as foretold by Ewan's stepfather, a Highland seer, to the fateful end as Ewan seeks to make his escape to exile in France. There is a slight sub-plot focused on love. The narrative concentrates on the fictional characters but historical characters also appear; the background is clear and generally accurate although little is made of the actual events of the battle of Culloden. The novel deals with such themes as honesty, loyalty to family and individual, truth, friendship and betrayal. The other two novels in the trilogy are *The Gleam in the North* and *The Dark Mile*.

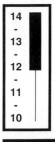

14
-
13
-
12
-
11
-
10

Highlands

Jacobites

Love

Loyalty

War

FRONTIER WOLF
Rosemary Sutcliff

Oxford, 1980 (op); Puffin, 1984, ISBN:0140314725 (op)

Alexios Aquila, a Roman centurion in disgrace after his loss of a fort in Germany, is sent to command a garrison of Frontier Scouts at the fort of Castellum (Cramond) on the border of Caledonia. The story deals with his success in gaining the trust of these irregular 'Frontier Wolves', and with how he deals with the local Celtic tribe and its chief. His efforts, however, end in failure when a major attack on Roman power erupts and he has to evacuate the fort and retreat south. The Romans have to withdraw completely from north of Hadrian's Wall, and a chapter of British history ends. The sense of a declining Roman Empire in the fourth century set against the growing confidence of the Celtic tribes is well created. The military details and the Celtic way of life are vividly described. This is a novel in the sequence about the Romano-British Aquila family that began with *The Eagle of the Ninth*.

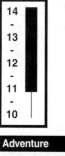

14
-
13
-
12
-
11
-
10

Adventure

Central Scotland

Romans

War

THE GLEAM IN THE NORTH
D.K. Broster
Heinemann, 1927 (op); in THE JACOBITE TRILOGY, Lomond Books, 1994, ISBN:1842040324

The second part of Broster's trilogy (begun with *The Flight of the Heron* and concluded by *The Dark Mile*) follows Ewan Cameron, his wife and family in the post-Culloden period. It is a dark, romantic tale of espionage, loyalty and betrayal, with a number of likely and unlikely suspects. The Jacobite Ewan is desperately trying to save his cousin, Dr Archie Cameron, from the government forces who repress the Highlands, and in the process he comes into contact with the family of the dead Keith Windham, his former Hanoverian prisoner. The scene shifts around various locations in Scotland and London, all very well realised in 18th century terms, and the action moves along at a pace. The characterisation follows that of the previous volume in credibility, with protagonists who are heroic and villainous without becoming caricatures who will appeal to a young readership. Although there is a background of real political events and historical figures, the novel does not allow these to dominate, and narrative is as strong as in *The Flight of the Heron*.

THE HERRING GIRLS
Theresa Tomlinson
Julia MacRae, 1994 (op); Red Fox, 1996, ISBN:0099363119

This novel is unique in using historic early photographs. Frank Sutcliffe's misty studies of the Whitby fishing community in Yorkshire in the 1880s are integrated into the narrative, and Sutcliffe himself features in the story as the 'picture man'. The story is worth reading in its own right as an account of a girl, Dory, who assumes adult responsibilities when hardship strikes her poor family. It justifies its place in this selection because of the part played by 'the Scotch lassies', the Herring Girls of the title. These itinerant teams of feisty young fish gutters pursue the herring fishing down the east coast of England. Tough and high-spirited, they show solidarity against exploitation by the merchants. At first they are hostile to the novice Dory and her friends because they suspect them of blacklegging. Sympathies grow, however, despite the unintelligibility of their dialect, and the Scots become role models for the other girls. Romantic attachments soon follow when fishermen and gutters meet at the Scotch lassies' ceilidh. Very effective dialogue should make an impact with younger readers.

KATE CRACKERNUTS
Katherine M Briggs
Alden Press, 1963 (op); Canongate Kelpies (abridged), 1987, ISBN:0862410967 (op)

This novel elaborates a traditional tale of two stepsisters, 'The Two Kates'. The period is Cromwell's invasion when Scotland has suffered grievously at the battles of Dunbar and Worcester. Action centres on Criffel in Galloway but extends to the Yorkshire Dales. Catherine, the beautiful daughter of the Laird of Auchenskeoch, and her hardy stepsister Kate endure and finally defeat the witchery of the laird's malevolent second wife, who is also Kate's mother. The story explores the omnipresence of the witch cult in the minds of remote peasant communities. Crucially, illness is a matter of evil spells and blessed charms. The reader also encounters the routines of a Border keep, and particularly the skills and responsibilities of womenfolk when the men are away at the wars. The enmities of rival families of Kennedys, Maxwells and Lindsays form another strand of the narrative. There is skilful characterisation of the tragically jealous stepmother, the laird torn between national and domestic worries, the contrasted Kates and their various suitors. This is a challenging novel for fluent older readers with some interest in Scottish history.

14
-
13
-
12
-
11
-
10

Borders

Feuds

Galloway

Witches

THE LAND THE RAVENS FOUND
Naomi Mitchison
Collins, 1955, (op); Black Knight Books, 1968, ISBN:0340039914 (op)

The story opens in a ninth century Norse settlement in Caithness. When Drostan the chief is fatally ambushed by Scots, his young son Anlaf must assume the role of leader. Aud the wise matriarch persuades the little community to quit their embattled territory for a new home in Iceland. There follow lively accounts of the building of the expedition's boat, of the strains of life at sea and the company's desperate attempt to make a safe landfall on Iceland. The group manages to settle and gradually prosper on the meagre shores of the Hvammafjord. Finally Aud hands over all her properties to Anlaf and dies contented on the night of his wedding feast. The novel offers a persuasive picture of the life of the Norse settlements in Caithness and Iceland. An underlying theme is the growth of the New Faith, Christianity, and its conflict with the pagan ways of the older warriors. Some young readers will certainly respond to the author's sympathy for the point of view of the womenfolk and of the Irish and Scots slaves captured in raids.

14
-
13
-
12
-
11
-
10

Dark Ages

Emigration

Seafaring

Vikings

14
13
12
11
10

Celtic tradition

Dark Ages

Loss

Loyalty

War

THE LAST HARPER
Julian Atterton
Julia Macrae, 1983 (op); Richard Drew, 1987, ISBN:0862671841 (op)

This historical novel based on old ballads deals with the struggle of the Celtic kingdoms of Southern Scotland and Northern England to survive against the invading Angles after the Roman withdrawal from Britain in the 5th century. When Gwion's father, harper to the king of the Votadini, is killed by the invaders, the young apprentice travels south with his wounded uncle Cailgrin, the blacksmith. In the kingdom of Rheged their skills are much appreciated, Gwion continuing his apprenticeship under the King's harper Myrddin, and Cailgrin making swords for the day when they will be needed in a battle of revenge against the 'Sea Wolves'. When the Celtic tribes finally manage to lay aside their differences against the common enemy, three great battles are won and final victory seems assured, until treachery and betrayal bring disaster. Gwion is left to tell the tales of victory and defeat.

This work offers convincing characters and a powerful story of upheaval and fear, dangerous journeys and savage battles. Dealing with themes of growing up, friendship, loss, loyalty, revenge and betrayal it really brings the past to life.

14
13
12
11
10

Adventure

Angus

Love

The sea

THE LIGHTHOUSE
R.M. Ballantyne
Thomas Nelson, 1865 (op)

The action occurs around Arbroath and the Bell Rock during the Napoleonic Wars, when Robert Stevenson is building his great lighthouse on the reef. The hero of the story is a stalwart, accident-prone lad, Ruby Brand, who has been wrongly accused of theft. On the run he hides away as a blacksmith with the squad working on the Bell Rock. His sweetheart Minnie, an eccentric uncle, two villainous smugglers, a stereotyped crew of navvies and Stevenson the engineer have supporting roles. The central personality is however the growing lighthouse as it triumphs over the elements.

The loose narrative wanders into the problems of building and living offshore. There are melodramatic adventures involving the pressgang, the Auchmithie caves and wrecking. Ruby and Minnie live happily ever after within sight of the beams of the light. Ballantyne spent a fortnight on the Rock and the outcome is a memorable curiosity; a primitive work of faction. It is not an easy read, being clumsy and at times bathetically pious. There are however able young readers who will be drawn to its untidy enthusiasms.

THE MARK OF THE HORSE LORD
Rosemary Sutcliff

Oxford University Press, 1965 (op); Puffin, 1983, ISBN:0140314733 (op)

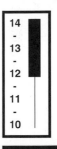

This historical novel is set in what is now Scotland in the last years of the Roman Empire in Britain. It deals with the tension between the Dalriads (Scots) and the Caledones (Picts) in the western territory now called Argyll, outside the Roman Empire. The Dalriads are Sun-worshippers, and their king is the Horse Lord; the Caledones worship the Great Mother, who is represented on earth by their Queen. The Dalriads, however, have lost their King and turned back to the old Caledonian ways under the influence of the King's half-sister, Liadhan, who rules as Queen. To secure her rule, she has blinded and exiled the true heir of the Horse Lord. Now some Dalriad chiefs are plotting to overthrow her, but they need a candidate for the role of Horse Lord. Fate gives them such a man. Phaedrus is a Roman slave of half-British parentage who has made his reputation as a gladiator and ultimately wins his freedom by killing a friend in the arena. Unable to handle his new state, he is ready to be enlisted as the instrument of a plan by the rebel Dalriads to install him as Horse Lord. This is made possible by the close resemblance he bears to the blinded Midir, the true heir. The story vividly recounts the adventures of Phaedrus as he follows this unexpected destiny to its powerful and gripping conclusion. The novel can be highly recommended; the difficulties in understanding the unfamiliar historical situation are quickly overcome in following a strong and clearly-told sequence of interesting events.

14 - 13 - 12 - 11 - 10

Adventure
Argyll
Celtic tradition
Dark Ages

A PISTOL IN GREENYARDS
Mollie Hunter

Evans, 1965 (op); Floris Kelpies, 2002, ISBN:0863154115

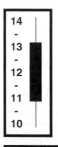

Mollie Hunter uses the brutal clearance of Greenyards in Sutherland in 1854 as the basis for this novel. The story is told by Connal Ross, a young boy from Greenyards, who puts up a spirited but ultimately futile resistance to the clearance of his glen. The women of Greenyards block the sheriff's entrance to the glen and tear up the writs of eviction. Caught up in the vicious attack which follows, Connal prevents the sheriff from shooting his mother by threatening him with an old pistol. The sheriff vows revenge and Connal becomes a fugitive from the law. When his mother is charged with murder, Connal leaves his mountain hideout and secures the help of a sympathetic lawyer who succeeds in having the charge dropped to breach of the peace and a one year sentence. With the sheriff on his trail he flees to Fort William and is smuggled aboard an emigrant ship. Mollie Hunter's skilful use of first person narrative draws the reader into the story and gives the central character some psychological depth. Connal, the proud, spirited and impulsive hero has to put behind him the bitterness of defeat and grasp the opportunity of a new life in America.

14 - 13 - 12 - 11 - 10

Adventure
Clearances
Emigration
Sutherland

33

THE POPINJAY
Iona McGregor
Faber & Faber, 1969 (op); Puffin, 1979, ISBN:0140310959 (op)

This novel starts in St Andrews in 1546 when the murder of Cardinal Beaton followed by plague have together created terror in the town. Into this situation steps a boy of sixteen, David Lindsay, returning after a year at his father's home in Bordeaux. He finds himself in a strange, uncouth country. With his fancy continental manners and clothes he justifies the nickname of Popinjay given to him by his former schoolmates in the town. He has to adjust to a new understanding of his fellow scholar, Martin, who has joined the Reformers, and he learns to value the old merchant who takes him in and the fisher girl, Elspeth. She is of his own age but more pragmatic and is able to help him as much as he helps her. Eventually they realise they are in love.

Fife

Growing up

Love

The Reformation

This book does require some knowledge of the historic events of the time and is not an easy read but interested readers will appreciate both the detailed setting and period and the lively action of the narrative. Although the ending is unashamedly romantic, the main narrative drive follows the dangers and alarms of the times and gives a flavour of what life was like. The reader ends up with considerable respect for our ancestors.

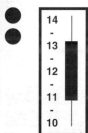

QUEST FOR A KELPIE
Frances Mary Hendry
Canongate Kelpies, 1986 (op); Floris Kelpies, 2002, ISBN:086241136X

Jeannie Main's defence of the tinker Margaret Davidson involves her in all kinds of trouble, not least the fighting between Jacobites and Hanoverians during the second Jacobite Rising, culminating in the Battle of Culloden. Margaret Davidson's mother, who has the sight, prophesies that Jeannie will meet her four times more in the shadow of the gibbet, will make a king and break a king, and will have to ride the kelpie to achieve what she wants in life. The tinkers' gratitude to Jeannie and her family gives Jeannie access to some of their lore, but she has to find the solution to her needs within herself. The kelpie of the title does not appear until the end of the narrative, but it is worth waiting for.

Adventure

Celtic tradition

Jacobites

Scots language

Supernatural

Like Mollie Hunter's novels, this is based on historical fact, and gives an excellent sense of the period. The language of the people of the north east is effectively rendered, but does not create a barrier to the reader.

QUEST FOR A MAID
Frances Mary Hendry

Canongate Kelpies, 1988 (op); Econo-Clad Books, 2001, ISBN:0613377001 (op)

This is an ideal novel for a south Fife reader, as it is set in and around Dunfermline. The family of Meg Rolfsdaughter lives in Inverkeithing, where Rolf is a shipwright. He builds the ship in which Sir Patrick Spens sails to Norway to collect the Maid, who is to marry the new king. Meg is a girl who stands up for herself, has a sharp and ready tongue, and only submits with a poor grace to the feminine ways expected of her. She is her father's favourite and gets away with a good deal. Her sister, Inge, is thought to be a white witch, but the first time that Meg witnesses her casting a spell, it is to cause the death of the king, Alexander III. This is the second strand of the story – the historical background including the trial of Inge as a witch when suspicion falls on her.

Quite a difficult read but a fascinating insight into life in Scotland in the thirteenth century, showing that Hendry has done her research thoroughly.

Family

Fife

Middle Ages

Seafaring

Witches

RAIDER'S TIDE
Maggie Prince

HarperCollins, 2002, ISBN:0007124031

This is the story of the first, forbidden love of young Beatrice Garth, daughter of the brutish squire of Barrowbeck Tower. In the 16th century England and Scotland regard each other as foreign, hostile nations. The place is the Kent estuary on Morecambe Bay where fortified farms and small communities live in constant alert against Scottish reivers slipping down through the Lakeland fells or by boat across the Solway. After a particularly lethal raid on the tower, Beatrice finds a young Scot left for dead and secretly tends to his wounds. As he recovers, they begin to fall in love. If the pair are found out, the Border penalty for him will be hanging and for her, burning at the stake. With Beatrice's drunken father addicted to highway robbery, she discovers that her mother is also finding solace in a dangerous liaison with the Cocklegatherer, a hermit-like medicine man. The narrative communicates vividly the domestic economy of Barrowbeck, giving a sense of the limited lives and prospects of the womenfolk. This fast-moving romance with its final feelings of lost love will be appreciated by older readers. Beatrice encounters further emotional and cross-border perils in *North Side of the Tree* (2003).

Borders

Family

Love

Reivers

35

REMEMBRANCE
Theresa Breslin
Doubleday, 2002; Corgi, 2003, ISBN:0552547387

Two families in a Borders village endure, and are forever changed by, the tragic impact of the First World War. Charlotte (15) and her older brother Francis live in Stratharden House: their widowed mother owns the local estate. John Malcolm, his sister Maggie and young Alex belong to a lower social stratum since their parents run the village shop. As the threat of war looms, romantic attachments grow tentatively between the young people across the barriers of the established order. In very different circumstances the three lads go off to war and their sisters work in munitions and hospitals. At the centre of the narrative is the shifting relationship between tough-minded Maggie the grocer's daughter and Charlotte the genteel girl with a natural talent for nursing. Both find war work hard but also liberating. Together they suffer the agonies of waiting for news from France. Which of the boys will perish and which survive? A striking feature of the narrative is the sequence of letters which give a graphic picture of the horrors of trench warfare. This is a vivid, demanding novel which older readers are likely to find deeply moving.

Borders
Class
Family
World War I

THE SHINING COMPANY
Rosemary Sutcliff
Bodley Head, 1990 (op); Red Fox, 2003, ISBN:0099439557

Prosper, a young Welsh squire, attended by his Irish servant Conn, follows Prince Gorthyn of Gwynedd as his shield-bearer to Dun Eidyn (Edinburgh). There the king of the Gododdin is gathering an elite company of warriors to march into the Saxon kingdoms of the south and break their power, which is threatening the security of the Celtic lands. The story follows their preparations, their march south to Catraeth (Catterick), and the disastrous battle that ends their hopes. The story is rather overloaded with Celtic detail, but is of interest because it deals with Britain after the departure of the Romans and the battles of Arthur against the invading Saxons. It is derived from the earliest surviving poem from what is now Scotland, the heroic elegy *The Gododdin*, dating from the seventh century and written in the Brythonic (or Welsh) variety of Celtic.

Celtic tradition
Dark Ages
Edinburgh
Heroism
War

THE SPANISH LETTERS
Mollie Hunter

Evans, 1964 (op); Floris Kelpies, 2003, ISBN:0863154123

It is 1589. D'Aquirre, the unscrupulous agent of King Philip of Spain, has conspired with the rebel Catholic Scottish earls Huntly, Crawford and others to permit a Spanish invasion, the capture of King James VI and ultimately the invasion of England. He has persuaded them to sign 'the Spanish Letters' committing them to this plot. A young English intelligence officer, a fencing master and his daughter, young Jamie Morton and his fellow caddies (the messenger brotherhood of Edinburgh) make common cause to forestall these happenings by acquiring the letters before they leave the country. They track down d'Aquirre and he is slain but the letters have already crossed the border in the hands of the servant of a renegade Scot. The Englishman, however, outrides him and the crisis is averted. In the meantime Huntly is on the point of kidnapping the King when he is thwarted by the magnificent march of the caddies who stir up the townspeople in the royal defence.

This story is carefully researched and historical facts are effortlessly conveyed. Above all it is a very exciting and gripping tale with its searches and chases through the wynds of 16th century Edinburgh. Especially exciting is the secret tunnel from the shore of the Nor Loch which takes Jamie into the old Guise Palace.

14
13
12
11
10

Edinburgh

Espionage

Love

THE STORY OF RANALD
Griselda Gifford

Bodley Head, 1968 (op); Canongate Kelpies, 1985, ISBN:0862410940 (op)

Based on fact, this account of refugees in the disastrous '45 rising starts in Keppoch, a remote Jacobite heartland north of Fort William. When Ranald's father, a MacDonald officer, is captured in battle and may be executed, his mother finds herself in charge of the household including her six small children. A cousin who has just fought at Culloden helps the family to flee south through the hills towards the safety of Rannoch moor, taking servants, cattle and dogs with them. This chaotic enterprise is the heart of the narrative. Eventually the children find safe houses in Edinburgh and the Borders. The focus is on ten-year-old Ranald, the only boy in the family. A timorous, delicate lad he learns painfully during the dangerous journey to assume manly responsibilities, but manages also to remain true to his own gentler feelings. By the time Ranald hears of his father's death, exile faces him, but he seems unwilling to follow in the family's warrior traditions. This quietly moving, accessible treatment of the plight of young refugees has a contemporary resonance which should interest thoughtful readers.

14
13
12
11
10

Growing up

Jacobites

Refugees

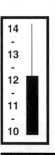

14
13
12
11
10

Family

Growing up

Orkney

Outsiders

Romans

THE STRONGHOLD
Mollie Hunter
Hamish Hamilton, 1974 (op); Canongate Kelpies, 1995, ISBN:0862415004 (op)

Some years before Julius Caesar's invasion of Britain, Roman raiding bands were a perennial danger to the tribes settled on the Orkney Islands and the northern mainland of Scotland. Coll lost his father and mother, and his own strength to one of these raids, and ever since has sought to find a means of safeguarding the tribe. His adoptive father, Nectan, the leader of the tribe of the Boar, and Domnall, the Chief Druid, are locked in conflict over the best way to fight the Romans, a conflict provoked by the newcomer Taran, who thirsts for power and is unconcerned how he gets it. Coll's idea for the stronghold, an eight-storey-high fortified tower which would be both a safe haven for the non-fighting members of the tribe and a launchpad for an effective riposte to raiding parties, is one he has to fight to achieve, risking the curse of Domnall to do so.

As is always the case with Hunter's novels, the reader has to attend and follow an adult treatment of plotting and characterisation, but will gain a vivid impression of a complex and vibrant community of individuals, as well as a reliable sense of developing history.

14
13
12
11
10

Adventure

Edinburgh

Growing up

French Revolution

THE TREE OF LIBERTY
Iona McGregor
Faber & Faber, 1972, ISBN:0571101216 (op)

Set in the stirring and dangerous times of the French revolution this is the story of the Lindsays, a prosperous Edinburgh family who have moved with the times from the old city to the New Town. However, they and especially their teenage children, Caroline and Sandy, cannot escape the arguments about liberty and equality that have spread all over Europe. The two children, one by escaping the limited society role expected of her and the other by taking direct action, show that the younger generation wish to contribute to a newer, fairer world. Their parents prove surprisingly helpful when the authorities catch up with Sandy and his life is threatened.

This is a carefully researched period novel, weaving the story of the fictitious Lindsays into the real history of Thomas Muir and Robert Watt, but focusing on the central brother and sister to let us see how real people must have felt and thought at that time. Well written with lively action and dialogue, it is an enjoyable human story.

THE WIDE BLUE ROAD
Marion Campbell

J.M. Dent, 1957 (op); revised version by Scottish Children's Press, 2002, ISBN:1899827846

14
-
13
-
12
-
11
-
10

Argyll

Middle Ages

Seafaring

Vikings

Richard, a young Norman noblemen rejected by his father, is enlisted as a page by a kindly Scottish knight who brings him to Dubhsgeir, a lochside stronghold in Knapdale in Argyll. The year is 1263, the period of the last great Norse campaign in Scotland. Old King Haakon's fleet is moving south to the Clyde in an attempt to re-establish Norwegian control. Richard finds himself caught up in the expedition with a girl Eithne and the treacherous Viking Ljuf. The rapidly moving adventure climaxes in a vigorous account of the storm-tossed and decisive battle of Largs. Its distinctive quality is a loving eye for historical authenticity. Knightly and heroic codes of behaviour are shown in action. Much of the activity takes place in boats. Characterisation is not complex but there is a colourfully varied cast of Normans, Scots, Norsemen and one Saracen. This is a readable and reliable fictionalising of one of the key events in Scottish history. In some schools, it might be read in conjunction with a class visit to the Vikingar Centre at Largs.

THE WONDER ON THE FORTH
Donald Lightwood

Scottish Children's Press, 1999, ISBN:1899827927

14
-
13
-
12
-
11
-
10

Bullying

Fife

Outsiders

Poverty

School

Like Lightwood's earlier *The Baillie's Daughter* this novel is strong in episodic social history. A simple, powerful story for younger and less confident readers, it takes place in Fife during the final construction stages of the Forth Bridge. The theme is the defiant survival of two motherless children whose father labours on the bridge. Brother and sister, they live primitively in a tent near the site. Their father, who is a good worker but vulnerable to drink, unthinkingly neglects them. At school the children experience both cruelty and kindness from their teachers. Bullied by their classmates as smelly outcasts they start truanting and are vindictively committed to the Dickensian horrors of the Dumfermline Poorhouse. They endure grim experiences including the trawling of a corpse of a navvy fallen from the bridge and the death of an aged pauper. But on the run again they also receive gentle kindness from a family of travelling folk who represent the old natural ways in contrast to the values symbolised by the great iron wonder. The two stick together and are reconciled with their father who finds a secure job – painting the new bridge.

14
-
13
-
12
-
11
-
10

Class

Clearances

Mystery

Skye

Supernatural

THE YEAR OF THE STRANGER
Allan Campbell McLean
Collins, 1971 (op); Floris Kelpies, 2002, ISBN:0862414857

This haunting novel focuses on the clearance township of Uig in Skye in 1877. Young Calum lives under sufferance in the house of his bigoted uncle, Tomas Caogach. His sister is in service at the Lodge which tyrannises the life of the glen. Calum stubbornly tries to help Mata the tinker who is stoned by the folk of the township. He also makes fleeting contact with the laird's young cousin, Lady Elizabeth, but the class gulf is unbridgeable.

An exotic visitor arrives mysteriously with his performing monkey. This Christlike stranger conjures an abundance of herring from the bay and associates with the outcast tinkers. He also brings retribution upon the diabolic factor. In the end however he is spurned by the community. The story's themes coalesce in an apocalyptic storm during which Calum penetrates the Uamh an Oir and achieves a vision of the glen as it might have been. In what seems a judgment floodwaters destroy the Lodge. Calum's vivid flash-back narrative incorporates biblical and folktale elements. Its ambiguities will promote differing interpretations among young readers.

PARA HANDY TALES
Neil Munro
William Blackwood & Sons Ltd, 1931 (op); Birlinn, 2002, ISBN:1841582271

Neil Munro began publishing his Para Handy stories as individual sketches in his 'Looker On' column of the *Glasgow Evening News* in 1905 and continued writing them for almost the rest of his life. The stories tell of the humorous adventures of the puffer *The Vital Spark* and her crew. Para Handy, her captain, is intensely proud of his craft – 'the smertest vessel in the coastin' tred – Oh man! She was the beauty! She was chust sublime!' – when in reality she has seen better days. Much of the humour stems from the rivalry between the members of the crew, two of whom are Highlanders and two are from the Lowlands. The stories are good fun, often displaying a subtle understated humour which sometimes verges on the surreal. In 'Treasure Trove' the crew decide to exploit a beached whale to supplement their income. In 'The Malingerer' three of the crew scare The Tar out of his laziness by convincing him that he is mortally ill. They can also be powerfully satirical. In 'Pension Farms' Munro highlights the danger of the newly introduced Old Age Pension being exploited to the detriment of the very people it was intended to benefit. The fact that these stories have never been out of print since their creator died in 1930 is testimony to their excellent and enduring quality.

14
13
12
11
10

Argyll

Clyde

Satire

Seafaring

PURE DEAD MAGIC
Debi Gliori
Doubleday, 2001; Corgi, 2002, ISBN:0552547573

Through this hilarious, elegantly concocted brew swirl traces of homage to *St Trinians*, *The Godfather*, *Dracula*, *Mary Poppins*, *Gormenghast*, *Harry Potter*, *The Addams Family* and *The Hitchhiker's Guide*. A Gothic schloss on an Argyll lochside is inhabited by the Strega-Borgias, a wildly dysfunctional trio of Saki-esque children, their feckless mother and a menagerie of lethal monsters and pets. These include a serially pregnant rat whose brood go to ground in the CD-ROM and get lost on the Net. A cryogenic ancestor fitfully sleeps out the centuries in the depths of the kitchen freezer. Helped by a lipstick-using spider and their witch-nanny the children try to teleport their father, the Count, out of Mafia clutches. All ends well, with the moat's crocodile turning vegetarian and the rat pregnant again. There is much ado with computer games and webs of one kind or another. The black and lavatorial fun is coloured by delicate lyrical touches. One can never be sure how relentlessly zany humour will take with children but the contemporary attitudes and idioms of this splendidly tall story seem likely to grab the attention. The Strega-Borgia clan survives further comic ordeals in *Pure Dead Brilliant* (2002) and *Pure Dead Wicked* (2003).

14
13
12
11
10

Computers

Family

Fantasy

Magic

Monsters

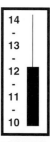

14
-
13
-
12
-
11
-
10

Family

Glasgow

Scots language

WEE MACGREEGOR
J.J. Bell

First published by the author, 1901 (op); Birlinn, 1998, ISBN:1874744092

The Robinsons are a decent working-class family who live up a tenement close in Glasgow at its late Victorian peak. There are two children, Macgregor (Wee Macgreegor) a pre-teenage urchin and his baby sister Jeannie. Their mother Lizzie is firmly in charge, with her husband indulging his son's hilarious mischief. In the background are grandparents, relatives and neighbours. The novel has its cosy sentimental moments, but Macgreegor is an enduring comic creation. His territory is domestic, extending into the city's streets and parks, with family visits, celebrations and sorties to Rothesay. He acts impetuously or with ingratiating cunning as the occasion prompts. He can be trusted to ask unanswerable 'Whit wey?' questions about the nature of things. He has the young animal's beady obsession with food ... *taiblet* in particular. He can usually, however, be brought to heel by Lizzie's favourite medical remedy and instrument of discipline, Castor Oil. In school the 24 bite-size escapades are ideal for dramatic activities and reading aloud. Self-contained, they exploit a rich Glaswegian Scots dialogue embedded in a narrative commentary in English.

ACROSS THE BARRICADES
Joan Lingard

Hamish Hamilton, 1972 (op); Puffin, 1995, ISBN:0140371796

This novel begins three years after *The Twelfth Day of July* and continues the story of Kevin and Sadie. Their relationship develops despite relentless opposition from their families and against a background of inter-community violence. Sadie is fired from her job for going out with a 'Mick' and Kevin is beaten up by three boys who call him a traitor. His situation becomes more and more difficult when an IRA supporter tries to involve him in terrorist activities. He is then framed by a jealous girl and is subsequently sacked by the girl's father. The young couple are befriended by Mr Blake, a former teacher of Sadie's, whose home becomes a temporary sanctuary for them. After Mr Blake is killed in a petrol bomb attack on his home, they feel terrible guilt and Kevin comes to the bitter realisation that there is no future for them in Belfast. Sickened by the violence, he decides to leave and try to find work in London. Sadie resolves to go with him. It is Joan Lingard's realistic portrayal of divided communities, her skilful building of narrative tension and her creation of an engaging hero and heroine which makes this the most satisfying of the five stories.

The story of Kevin and Sadie after they leave Belfast continues in *Into Exile* (1973), *A Proper Place* (1975) and *Hostages to Fortune* (1976).

14
-
13
-
12
-
11
-
10

Growing up

Northern Ireland

Outsiders

Sectarianism

I'LL GO MY OWN WAY
Mollie Hunter

Hamish Hamilton, 1985 (op); Fontana, 1987, ISBN:0006726372 (op)

This teenage novel introduces a memorable heroine, Cat McPhie, the only child of a family of travelling people. Their traditional way of life is challenged by the pressures of the modern world, both from outwith the community (in the shape of police and local harassment) and from within it (in the attractions of dealing in cars and other machines). Cat's parents have brought her up individualistically: her father has passed on to her the skills of poaching and river pearling traditionally reserved for males, and her mother has passed on to her elements of her own 'second sight'. From both, she has learned to be forthright and independent, and much of the personal conflict of the novel arises from her desire to preserve a traditional travelling life, but not within a traditional marriage to Charlie Drummond, who has her 'marked down' as his woman. Their final negotiation of a loving relationship balances some haunting and tragic scenes, as the travellers' camp is set on fire by a gang of disaffected youths.

14
-
13
-
12
-
11
-
10

Family

Supernatural

Travelling folk

14
-
13
-
12
-
11
-
10

Growing up

Northern Ireland

Outsiders

Sectarianism

INTO EXILE
Joan Lingard
Hamish Hamilton, 1973 (op); Puffin, 1995, ISBN:014037213X

Newly married, in poorly paid jobs and living in a rented room in a rundown London street, Kevin and Sadie have to adjust to a new way of life. Both are homesick and Sadie, in particular, feels isolated and lonely. On the point of returning to Ulster, they are deterred by news of bombing in their own communities. They have arguments about money, Kevin's devout Catholicism, and the situation in Ulster. When Kevin's father is killed in a pub bombing, Kevin returns home to look after his family. Torn between the demands of his needy family, and his love for Sadie, Kevin agonises about what he should do. Isolated in London Sadie feels deserted and blames all their troubles on Kevin's religion. Gradually they work out their feelings in a series of letters. Realising how much she loves him, Sadie returns to Ulster at Kevin's request and Kevin, realising that he must make a choice between his family and Sadie, chooses Sadie. Once again they decide to leave Ulster and start afresh. Although this novel does not have the narrative drive of *Across the Barricades*, Joan Lingard's sensitive portrayal of the young couple's strong but troubled relationship gives it psychological depth.

14
-
13
-
12
-
11
-
10

Growing up

Northern Ireland

Outsiders

Sectarianism

THE TWELFTH DAY OF JULY
Joan Lingard
Hamish Hamilton, 1970 (op); Puffin, 1996, ISBN:0140372369

Set in the late 1960s this story tells of the exploits of Kevin McCoy, a Catholic boy and Sadie Jackson, a Protestant girl in the days leading up to the Twelfth of July. Kevin ventures into Protestant territory and paints 'Down with King Billy' under the mural on the Jackson's gable end. This leads to his first encounter with Sadie who retaliates with an anti-Catholic slogan on a wall in Kevin's street. These childish escapades, however, develop into vicious fighting. When Kevin's sister, Brede, is seriously injured by a brick, Sadie comes to her senses and runs to help Brede. Shocked that their childish escapades have escalated into such violence, Sadie refuses to take part in the Orange Walk on the Twelfth and instead, tries to visit Brede in hospital. The story ends optimistically when Kevin, Sadie and her brother become friends and spend the day together in Bangor. Joan Lingard skilfully portrays the claustrophobic streets of Belfast with their back-to-back houses and sectarian murals and develops the exploits of her young and spirited hero and heroine into a well-paced narrative which conveys a message of tolerance and reconciliation without preaching.

A FLUTE IN MAYFERRY STREET
Eileen Dunlop

Oxford University Press, 1976 (op); Floris Kelpies, 2000, ISBN:0863153283

14
-
13
-
12
-
11
-
10

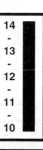

Edinburgh

Family

History

Supernatural

There is a ghostly element in this narrative, but it is predominantly a mystery, where the two Ramsay children, Marion and Colin, have to become detectives to find out what happened to the trunk which vanished from their house in 1914. At the beginning of the novel there is an atmosphere of sadness, as their father died suddenly of a heart attack, leaving the family ill-provided for, and then Marion was paralysed after a road accident. Finding out about Charles Ramsay and his friend Alan Farquhar gives Marion in particular something to interest her, and, although the clues are frustratingly small, difficult to understand and appear only after long periods of inactivity, they gradually allow the family to piece together events of more than 70 years before.

The ending, which could have been mawkish and sentimentalised, is surprisingly moving and effective, as all the bits of the jigsaw are finally fitted together and the whole story told. There is absolutely no concession on Dunlop's part to a child's lack of imagination or vocabulary, which makes this novel as enjoyable to the adult reader as to the young teenager.

THE GREAT ADVENTURES OF SHERLOCK HOLMES
Sir Arthur Conan Doyle

Puffin, 1995, ISBN:014036689X

14
-
13
-
12
-
11
-
10

Adventure

Crime

History

London

This selection contains eight of the Holmes stories. Some, such as *The Red-Headed League*, are well known and others are less familiar. All have the same format: the clever detective Holmes and his ally and recorder, the simple but honest Dr. Watson, meet wicked and insoluble mysteries which Holmes solves by logical, if sometimes extremely implausible, deductions. The stories have plenty of action as the protagonists leap into hansom cabs and trains at every opportunity and they are always facing deadlines and astonishing coincidences and barriers. There is a great deal of the 'You are mad!' 'Not a second to lose!' style of dialogue. No need for even a stupid detective to work out why they are popular with children of all ages. Puffin books also do three other Holmes books and an edition of *The Lost World*.

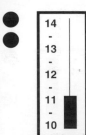

14
-
13
-
12
-
11
-
10

Change

Friendship

Supernatural

Thriller

PHANTOM FROM THE PAST
Neil Gavin

Jarrold, 1988, ISBN:0711703582 (op)

When a tragic skiing accident in the Canadian Rockies kills their parents, Robert and Fiona Mathieson move to Scotland to live with their Aunt Isobel in Perth where they have to begin a new way of life. They soon discover that not everyone is as welcoming as their aunt, though even she has her secrets. Dangerous adventures and menacing characters lie in wait for them as they set about trying to solve the puzzle of their true identity and get to the root of their father's dying words, 'remember you're a Kinlochy.' Robert's quest takes an even more sinister turn when the town is covered in fog and his sister is kidnapped by the Whisperer, an evil adversary who starts to haunt their lives, but Fiona has inherited the power of second sight and their friend Benjamin is a genius. The mystery continues in the sequel, *The Phantom Claymore.*

An enjoyable thriller mystery, with enough suspense, menacing characters and scary situations to suit young readers, though the main characters do seem a little precocious and the suspense contrived at times.

14
-
13
-
12
-
11
-
10

Clydebank

Friendship

Supernatural

World War II

THINK ME BACK
Catherine Forde

House of Lochar, 2001, ISBN:1899863788

Think Me Back is set on the anniversary of the worst night of the Clydebank Blitz. Pete Smeaton and his family have moved to Clydebank from London. In his new home he hears voices, particularly that of a young girl, coming through the wall from the adjoining house – but it no longer exists since it was destroyed by a bomb during the war. He and a local boy use an abandoned air raid shelter as their den. There they find further confirmation of the existence of the young girl who had lived in the house next door. She and Pete start to communicate, causing Pete to be transported back to the time of the Blitz on a number of occasions and in the shelter he experiences first hand the night the house was bombed. Eventually Pete understands why Beth comes back each year. Not only that, he meets her in his own time zone – an old woman aged about 70.

This story is taut and full of realism, humour, tension and mystery. It sees life through the eyes of modern child and recreates the tragedy of the Blitz. A plausible 'explanation' for the supernatural events is included, which should provoke discussion.

THE VALLEY OF DEER

Eileen Dunlop

Oxford University Press, 1989, ISBN:0192715992 (op)

Anne Farrar is the rather lonely, bookish girl trapped for a summer in The Owls' House in the Valley of Deer while her archaeologist parents excavate a Neolithic burial cairn before the valley is flooded for the new reservoir. When Anne finds a box containing a family bible dating from the seventeenth century with an intriguing reference to Alice Jardyne, she determines to find out who she was and why such a terrible fate should have been hers. The finding of a small, silver-bound crystal in the Neolithic mound deepens the mystery, but also appears to give Anne access to special knowledge about Alice. As the narrative progresses, and Anne learns more about Alice Jardyne, she allows herself to be taken over by her imagination (or by the spirit of Alice – the truth of the matter is debated throughout the novel) and undergoes a horrifying experience in the old Witch's Cottage in Hoolets' Wood where she supposes that Alice was lynched by her neighbours.

As in Dunlop's other novels of this type, the central character learns a great deal about herself, life and those around her from the influence of the past, and emerges stronger for the experience. An exciting, thought-provoking read, for the upper end of the age-range.

14
-
13
-
12
-
11
-
10

Highlands

History

Supernatural

Witches

47

OUTSIDERS

14
-
13
-
12
-
11
-
10

Creativity

Island life

Nature

School

THE BOY FROM SULA
Lavinia Derwent
Victor Gollancz, 1973 (op); Floris Kelpies, 2002, ISBN:086315400X

Magnus Macduff, the boy from Sula, has an intense and creative relationship with his Hebridean home, its people and its animals, particularly the seals. His special gifts as a painter help Magnus catch the essence of this island world, but also distance him from it when he is sent off to high school on the mainland. There he stays with the eccentric Duke of Cronan Castle, another isolated yet creative person. Sula is threatened by a London developer who wants to establish a holiday resort there, but accident and the spell of the island combine to thwart him. Magnus survives a serious head injury when swimming with the seals, but returns from hospital with a more mature sense of his community. The sequel to *Sula*, this haunting story for young readers blends folktale and quaintly comic fiction, and its evocation of a distant way of life fits well within its atmosphere of fable.

14
-
13
-
12
-
11
-
10

Humour

Love

Seafaring

THE CHINA RUN
Neil Paterson
Hodder & Stoughton, 1948 (op); Richard Drew, 1986, ISBN: 0862671469 (op)

Neil Paterson's novella tells the most extraordinary story behind two portraits of his great-grandmother, Christian West: one of an elderly, respectable burgess's wife, the other a glamorous exotic beauty. Brought up in a strictly religious family in the Northeast town of Banff in the early 19th century, Christian was virtually sold into marriage at the tender age of 16 to the 42 year old Captain of a visiting ship. However, by the time of his death 11 years later, she had not only mastered the arts of navigation and sailing, but learned to skipper the ship with a combination of feminine guile and firm discipline, outmanoeuvred ruthless dealers and avaricious relatives of her late husband, fought off drunken sailors, Chinese pirates and above all the bold Tancy McCoy, an American skipper who pursued her obsessively across the seven seas. Fascinating central character, gripping, humorous storyline about the role of women in a male-dominated society.

DEAR DEL
Alison Prince
Hodder & Stoughton, 2001, ISBN:0340851570

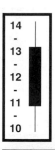

The action takes place over one summer week on the island of Broray, which is clearly Arran on the Firth of Clyde. Fran is a teenager whose incomer family runs the village shop at the north end of the island. She has been having difficulties adjusting to the local High School and now finds herself faced with the problem of putting in the time with an unresponsive visitor. Del, a deprived, damaged girl from a Glasgow housing scheme, has been sent by a charitable agency for a week's holiday on the island. Vulnerable despite her hard carapace, she finds herself out of her depths in Fran's well-intentioned family. She triggers a sequence of delinquencies including spray painting, shoplifting, and a mountain accident. Jolly visits planned to local attractions are mostly failures – a distillery, standing stones, a National Trust castle, and a hotel swimming pool. Gradually however the week proves to be a turning point for both girls as they confront their prejudices and dilemmas. This is a brief, neatly handled first-person narrative with effective dialogue. Its contemporary flavour should appeal to young readers.

14
-
13
-
12
-
11
-
10

Arran

Family

Island life

Prejudice

DON'T FORGET TO REMEMBER
Donald Lightwood
Scottish Children's Press, 1998, ISBN:1899827560

When the drama teacher sets Sandy the task of researching a mining disaster in which his grandfather was killed, the boy finds that digging up the past is not always welcome, especially in his own family. His contact with Auld Wattie, the village scapegoat and outcast, unearths deep wounds and secrets which Sandy's father and grandmother would prefer kept in the dark. Through his developing friendship with Wattie and the tensions this causes within the family, Sandy learns how dangerous and difficult it can be trying to explore the painful truths about human relationships. His grandmother is forced to face up to the past, and his unemployed father comes to terms with the truth about his dead father and his changing relationship with Sandy. In the end, forgiveness and reconciliation might just be possible for everyone concerned.

14
-
13
-
12
-
11
-
10

Family

Friendship

Mining

Prejudice

Unemployment

This is a story of family secrets, loyalties and tensions set in a modern mining community where the pit has closed and unemployment is high. It offers a strong storyline, and realistic characters and relationships. It deals with issues of identity and inheritance, prejudice and victimisation, lies and truth, forgiveness and redemption.

49

14
-
13
-
12
-
11
-
10

Bullying

Divorce

Family

Friendship

Glasgow

EVERYBODY DESERVES ONE GOOD DAY
Hugh Gillespie
Hodder & Stoughton, 1995, ISBN:034063913X

Joanne is an overweight twelve-year-old still struggling to come to terms with her parents' divorce, her mother's remarriage and the new baby. She feels she is completely taken for granted by her harassed mother as well as by her older sister and brother, who are too busy with boyfriend and football. If only she could have a new mountain bike for her birthday, like many of her friends, she would feel more loved and appreciated, but money is short and there are more pressing priorities. Temptation is put in her way, especially by the local bike thieves, but she discovers it is better to earn what she desires through her own initiative, a little luck and some help from her friends. She also realises that everybody deserves one good day at least, a day that draws the family back together and makes everyone feel more valued. Set in Glasgow this novel has realistic characters, problems and a sense of humour most teenagers will warm to. Though the language is occasionally demanding, the storyline is not.

14
-
13
-
12
-
11
-
10

Change

Edinburgh

Loss

School

THE HIGH HOUSE
Honor Arundel
Hamish Hamilton, 1967 (op); Canongate Kelpies, 1993, ISBN:0862414202 (op)

In the first novel in the trilogy, Emma and Richard's secure world is thrown into turmoil after the death of their parents and they each go to live with an aunt. Unfortunately both end up living with the aunt whose personality would have better suited the other child. Sensible Emma lived in Edinburgh with her unconventional Aunt Patsy, but her musical brother Richard in Exeter stayed with the more conventional and respectable Aunt Laura. *The High House* concentrates on Emma trying to find her way in a strange new world, living at the top of a dark tenement on the Royal Mile, coping with her 'weird' aunt's untidy habits and artistic temperament and at first wishing she was living with the other aunt, but gradually she and Aunt Patsy adjust to each other's ways and a new bond starts to develop. To her surprise, she also starts to love the dingy old town, make new friends at school and even cope with ogrish teachers. Decision time looms when Patsy and her boyfriend Stephen decide to get married and her legal guardian Aunt Laura, who would prefer to have the well-behaved Emma, arrives in Edinburgh along with her brother Richard for a summit conference on their futures.

THE MAGIC CHANTER
Sheila Douglas
Scottish Children's Press, 1997, ISBN:1899827102

Nine year old Iain Barlass who lives in Perth has the gift of the second sight, empowering him to see figures from the city's past. On a school trip into the Highlands, he brings the past to life as he meets people evicted from Gleann a' Chadail (the Sleepy Glen) during the Highland Clearances and learns from the piper Seamus Dhu of the curse on his family and their lost treasure. Through his friendship with the tinkers Lizzie and Geordie Black and their gift of the magic chanter, Iain is able to travel back and forward in time to unlock the curse, search for the lost treasure and be granted a vision of how the glen could be regenerated after its long sleep.

As well as being a good story, drawing on both Scots and Gaelic legend and folk tale, this is a historical fantasy with a message about how we can not only learn from the past, but also create a sustainable future by using and adapting the resources we have around us for the benefit of the whole community.

14
-
13
-
12
-
11
-
10

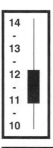

Clearances

Friendship

Perth

Quest

Supernatural

THE ROUGH ROAD
Margaret MacPherson
Collins, 1965 (op); Canongate Kelpies, 1988, ISBN:0862411777 (op)

MacPherson's very authentic Skye novels could well be read as a pair. Crofting in the Depression of the 1930s presents a harsher environment than that of the author's earlier *The Shinty Boys*. 13 year-old Jim lives in the care of foster parents who routinely maltreat him. Hardy but vulnerable, he channels his desperate insecurity into a fascination for cattle keeping. Gradually he develops an admiring friendship with Alastair, a foot-loose drover who initiates him in the cattleman's craft but also exploits the boy's eagerness to learn. When Alastair is felled by a maddened heifer on the Kyleakin slipway, Jim finds himself committed single-handed to herding 44 beasts by ferry and rail to the mart at Dingwall. He succeeds triumphantly but near-fatal trouble with his foster parents alienates him and drives him to live rough. He feels betrayed by his hero, but hopeful resolution finally emerges. This novel is distinguished by sensitive characterisation of the boy and those around him, including his crazed foster mother and the kindly but manipulative Alastair. The author has an eye for the idiosyncrasies of dogs and cattle.

14
-
13
-
12
-
11
-
10

Crofting

Drovers

Growing up

Skye

14
13
12
11
10

Adventure

Bullying

Growing up

Thriller

RUN, ZAN, RUN
Cathy Macphail
Blackie, 1994 (op); Bloomsbury, 2001, ISBN:0747555044

Katie Cassidy is a 13 year old child with a happy, normal home life but with a big problem at school. She is bullied by Ivy Toner and her pals. After Katie is driven to tell on Ivy at school, Ivy and her mates start threatening Katie out of school, so Katie tries to hide by going to places where the other girls do not play. One of these is the local dump. Here it is that Ivy tracks her down but is surprised when a hard, dirty girl emerges from a large cardboard box in which she has been staying and drives off Katie's tormentors. She won't give her name, so Katie thinks of her as 'Zan', the name on the box. Zan has her own reasons for hiding and coming to Katie's aid has consequences for her in which they all become involved in a fast, exciting tale which never lets up. The world of this book is one of continual arguments, of always having to watch your back and of never knowing who to trust, a rather noisy thriller in fact, and well deserving of the praise that has been heaped on it since its first publication.

14
13
12
11
10

Adventure

Growing up

Highlands

History

THE SASSENACH
Helen B. McKenzie
Canongate, 1980 (op); Canongate Kelpies, 1986, ISBN:0862411157 (op)

This story, set in the early 19th century, is full of action and excitement. Elspeth Maclaine, called a Sassenach by her classmates in their Highland village because she was born in England, becomes involved in her father's brushes with the law, partly because of illegal whisky and partly because of a rash of sheep stealing. Poor crofters who break the law in order to alleviate their poverty are set up by criminals and those with scores to settle, so Elspeth finds out that those she thinks are her friends may not be so, and those she fears may turn out to be saviours. She is also warned by Blind Betsy who has the second sight but understands the warnings too late.

The book gives a picture of the whole community including the dominie, the minister and the officers of the law but the focus is on the life of Elspeth, her parents and their problems, her friend Rory and his dog Ben. There is humour as well as fear and excitement. At the end of the story, of course, she is no longer 'the sassenach'.

SHADOW OF THE STONE
Catherine Lucy Czerkawska
Richard Drew, 1989, ISBN:0862672597 (op)

Liz Finlay, a rebellious teenager who often seeks refuge at the Granny Kempock stone which stands above Gourock, is haunted by the fate of Marie Lamont, a local girl burned as a witch in the 17th century. Liz is struggling to come to terms with her parents' divorce and her mother's relationship with a new boyfriend: neither of them approves of her obsession with sailing, especially when she develops an infatuation with Steve, a visiting American sailor on the track of his grandfather's sailing ship, *The Marie Lamont*. She has to free herself from the shadows of the past and the present, and is helped by her friend Tom, her grandmother Rose and Steve who teaches her not only to sail, but also to believe in herself and not rely too much on others.

This novel has complex central character and relationships, a strong storyline and themes to which most teenagers will relate.

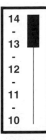

14
-
13
-
12
-
11
-
10

Clydeside
Divorce
Fantasy
History
Sailing

SOUNDTRACK
Julie Bertagna
Mammoth, 1999, ISBN:0749729805 (op)

This confident, multi-layered story portrays the isolation of a boy in a small coastal community. Finn goes to great lengths to engage with as few people as possible. He trusts only his uncle, and certainly not himself. The restless sea with its potential to delight and destroy fascinates him, blanking out the rest of his life and any thoughts about the future. When his beloved uncle drowns as a result of a terrible accident, the nets of his fishing boat caught by a submarine, he realises he can no longer hide and that he has a role and responsibilities in the shattered community. The location is not named and there are no obvious accents but the theme is universal because disasters, big and small, hit communities everywhere. Yet it is undoubtedly Scottish. The atmosphere, the influences, the heart and soul of the book are all Scottish without it ever being stated.

The title *Soundtrack* is vital to the story. Music is the soundtrack to Finn's life. It reflects his mood, expresses his feelings and vocalises his emotions. The contemporary groups mentioned will be of interest to readers and offer an interesting way to track the events and emotions of the novel through the lyrics.

14
-
13
-
12
-
11
-
10

Community
Loss
Music
The sea

THE SPARK GAP
Julie Bertagna
Mammoth, 1996, ISBN:0749727039 (op)

Set in Glasgow, this novel tells the tale of a group of young people who fall into homelessness. It is a powerful evocation of the isolation that results when communication breaks down, in this case as a result of a death in the family. Kerri chooses to live on the roof of a Glasgow tower block rather than the so-called security of the home her mother is offering. On that roof Mauve the artist and Skip, a boy who has built an almost impenetrable barrier between him and all outside influences, befriend her. This is the story of their extraordinary life together and the relationships that develop as a result of the chance meeting on the rooftop. This hard-hitting story shows how powerful teenagers can be. Even this disenfranchised trio discovers that relationships count for a great deal.

When vandals burn the tower block the trio go up to the north of Scotland on the proceeds of the sale of some of Mauve's pictures. The young people are soon bored, with the exception of Mauve who has her painting to sustain her, and embark on a fairly disastrous expedition, caused by their ignorance of the countryside and the weather conditions and a possible supernatural encounter on the moor. Kerri eventually returns to her mother who is working towards a more stable relationship with her daughter. Readers are left with the feeling that this relationship is precarious to say the least, but that both parties have learned from their recent experiences and are willing to work to help them succeed.

SULA
Lavinia Derwent
Gollancz, 1969 (op); Floris Kelpies, 2002, ISBN:0862410681

The fictional Sula is one of the remoter Hebridean Small Isles. Though suited to readers in the later primary stages, this novel in some ways anticipates Mairi Hedderwick's vivid picture narratives of Struay for much younger children. Set in the early 60's it employs an unusual blending of whimsical fun and quite stark realism. Magnus is an orphaned loner, an apparently sullen school refuser, who prefers the companionship of a seal and an unkempt recluse to the youngsters in Sula's one-teacher primary school. Although wilfully backward in his school subjects Magnus has a striking artistic talent and is fiercely absorbed in sketching the island's wild life. His provocative conflict with the newly appointed, frail young teacher is slowly resolved through episodes involving the arrival of a visiting yacht and a perilous gale. The supporting cast include a spartan grandmother, a comically ineffectual parish minister and Magnus's classmates, who bear more than a passing resemblance to some of Richmal Crompton's little monsters. The tale shifts uncertainly between caricature and melodrama, but there is strength and originality in the portrayal of changing relationships between Magnus and his inexperienced teacher. Magnus's story continues in *The Boy from Sula*.

THE WITCH'S DAUGHTER
Nina Bawden
Gollancz, 1966 (op); Puffin, 1973, ISBN:014030407X

This intriguing variant on the summer adventure yarn will suit confident readers. The plot skilfully weaves three familiar elements. An English family holidaying on the fictional Hebridean island of Skua encounters thieves trying to retrieve the loot of a London jewel robbery after the police manhunt has subsided. Both groups become involved in the predicament of a fey local orphan said to be a 'witch girl'. This key character, Perdita, is a 10-year old illiterate loner who does not attend school and lives in a derelict manse with an old woman. Her island peers are afraid of the ragged girl because she is said to have the second sight. As the narrative develops, the personalities of children, parents and villains acquire depths and individuality. Janey, the youngest of the visiting family, is blind but independent and tough-minded, whereas Tim her sighted brother is a dreamer suspected of romanticising events. When the children are abandoned in a Staffa-type sea cave it is blind Janey who can lead them through the darkness to safety. A quality of vulnerability accompanies Perdita to the novel's enigmatic conclusion.

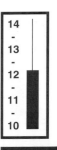

14
-
13
-
12
-
11
-
10

Crime

Hebrides

Supernatural

YOU CAN'T KISS IT BETTER
Diana Hendry
Red Fox, 2003, ISBN:0099403471

This moving and entertaining novel tells of of a small group of disturbed children and their foster mother, Megan. It brings to life the support services responsible for the care of vulnerable young people – social workers, teachers, Children's Panel, and police. The story is presented mainly by 12-year-old Anna. Wounded by her parents' desertion she is alert, confiding and prone to wishful fantasy. Her lively account is interspersed with a variety of diary entries, letters, school essays, and e-mails which reveal how others see things. The foster home is set on the Water of Leith in Edinburgh, and the changing seasonal life of the little river runs through the narrative as a lyrical, liberating force sometimes friendly, sometimes threatening the children. There are glancing references to The River in *The Wind in the Willows*. The episodes are short and direct; vivid key moments include a 'taking and driving away' incident; a Children's Panel review meeting, and a tumultuous spring flood on the river. There are no facile answers to the problems of these youngsters: 'You can't kiss it better'. After a few months three of the four have moved on, for reasons happy or sad. In a defiantly optimistic ending Anna sends a loving message in a bottle down the river in the hope that it will find her lost friend Brent.

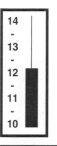

14
-
13
-
12
-
11
-
10

Edinburgh

Fostering

Humour

Loss

SCIENCE FICTION & FANTASY

THE BIG HOUSE
Naomi Mitchison

Faber & Faber, 1950 (op); Canongate Kelpies, 1987, ISBN:0862411599 (op)

It is 1945, the first Halloween after the lifting of blackout restrictions. The cantrips of Kintyre guisers trigger an elaborate time-shift rescue story which deploys folk motifs: Tam Lin, True Thomas, the perilous Queen of Fairy, the changeling, the lost piper, the benevolent Brounie and the swan maiden. The action moves confidently from the austerities of post-war rationing to the political unrest of the 1790s and further back to the Lordship of the Isles. It ranges across the peninsula, culminating in the fort on Dunadd.

The protagonists are Sue, the upper-class 12-year-old from the Big House which has always controlled the district; and her classmate Winkie, a boy from a fisher family in the village. Wayward and questioning, Sue probably represents how the author saw herself as girl. An emphatic theme is the changing but unpleasant realities of class affecting the lives of the gentry, the village folk and an outcast clan of Argyll tinklers. The narrative skilfully uses a colouring of Gaelic, Scots and Travellers' Cant. A highly original, uncondescending fusion of mythology, social history and the psychology of a childhood friendship.

Argyll

Celtic tradition

Class

History

Magic

EXODUS
Julie Bertagna

Picador, 2002, ISBN:0330400967

Set in 2100, this is an ambitious, complex Glasgow fable of global warming and flooding. It is rich in symbolic echoes and quirkily apt allusions to the legend of the city's coat of arms. Living on Wing a remote northern island (Hoy in Orkney?), Mara the young heroine becomes identified with the Pictish Princess Theneu who was cast adrift by her father but gave birth to Mungo, founding saint of Glasgow. As the narrative unfolds, Mara unwillingly recognises that her destiny is to rescue the inhabitants of a new city from waves and slavery. Her mission has three stages: evacuating Wing as the Atlantic rises; arriving among boat refugees in the horrors of sunken Glasgow; and overthrowing the gleaming dystopic world of New Mungo. The polluted netherworld of the old city is vividly realised, with rising tides encroaching on its north slope from the Necropolis to the University. The tyrannically corrupt sky city of New Mungo, which offers hi-tech luxury to its elite, towers above on massive columns. Permeating all is the anarchic, liberating medium of cyberspace. This absorbing novel handles large themes and is well worth the effort for confident older readers.

Computers

Glasgow

Global warming

Quest

Refugees

HARRY POTTER AND THE PHILOSOPHER'S STONE

J.K. Rowling

Bloomsbury, 1997, ISBN:0747532745

The first in the series, this book introduces the key characters that will participate in the books. Harry Potter, aged 11, lives with his aunt, uncle and cousin. Orphaned as a baby, he believes his parents died in a car crash. Harry is incredibly badly treated by his relatives and he has no real understanding of why this should be so. The adventure starts when, on his eleventh birthday he, eventually, receives a letter that invites him to take up his place in Hogwarts School of Witchcraft and Wizardry. Hagrid, the Keeper of the Keys at Hogwarts, delivers the letter. It is from Hagrid that Harry learns his true heritage. He is a wizard, the son of a witch and wizard who died trying to protect Harry from the evil wizard Voldemort. Harry himself survived the attack by Voldemort having managed to destroy him and with only a lightning scar on his forehead to show for it.

What follows is an adventure story in which strange events entangle Harry and his friends Ron Weasley and Hermione Granger. Clearly an evil presence is afoot and it transpires that Voldemort, designed to become Harry's arch enemy, is attempting to return to the world and seeks the philosopher's stone which will allow the bearer to live forever. Along the way Harry learns to play 'quidditch', meets teachers who will have a huge impact on his life, Professor McGonagall, Professor Snape and Professor Dumbledore, and encounters another pupil, Draco Malfoy, who presents as a more earthly rival throughout the course of events. During the course of the novel Harry learns to be self-sufficient and self-confident in a way he has not been able to do before. He is no longer a 'victim'.

14
-
13
-
12
-
11
-
10

Adventure

Magic

School

Wizards

HARRY POTTER AND THE CHAMBER OF SECRETS

J.K. Rowling

Bloomsbury, 1999, ISBN:0747538484

Harry returns for his second year at Hogwarts following his spectacular success in defeating Voldemort for a second time. His return to school is not straightforward. He is warned by Dobby, a house elf, not to return and he and Ron are prevented from catching the Hogwarts express and have to make their way to school using an illegal flying car. Central to this tale is the new Defence against the Dark Arts teacher, Professor Gilderoy Lockheart. Strange attacks begin to occur at the school and Harry, by being in the wrong place at the wrong time, becomes a prime suspect. A warning message is daubed on the wall saying, 'The Chamber of Secrets has been opened'. Lockheart claims to be able to get to the bottom of the mystery but it is Harry, Hermione and Ron who once again solve the puzzle. Readers are given more background information about Harry (he is a Parselmouth, one who can speak to snakes) and Voldemort, who as his alter ego Tom Riddle attended Hogwarts himself as a boy.

14
-
13
-
12
-
11
-
10

Adventure

Magic

School

Wizards

14
-
13
-
12
-
11
-
10

Adventure

Magic

School

Wizards

HARRY POTTER AND THE PRISONER OF AZKABAN
J.K. Rowling
Bloomsbury, 2000, ISBN:0747546290

Harry's return to Hogwarts for his third year is precipitated by his illegal use of magic on his Aunt Marge after being provoked by remarks about his parents. Concerned about the consequences of this, Harry flees the Dursley's home and makes his way, via the Knight bus, to Diagon Alley. There he is met by Cornelius Fudge, the Minister for Magic, who seems unconcerned with the reasons for Harry's hurried departure and more concerned with his safety. The escape of Sirius Black from Azkaban, the notorious wizard's prison, appears to be at the root of this and Harry learns that Black is supposed to have killed thirteen people on the night Harry's parents were killed and that he is thought to be one of Voldemort's supporters. Harry is considered to be a target for Black.

On the journey to the school the train is stopped and boarded by Dementors, the guards from Azkaban, beings that leach the happiness out of people, supposedly trying to find Black. Harry reacts very strongly to the Dementors and is protected by Professor Lupin the new Defence Against the Dark Arts teacher. The stage is set for another adventure for Harry and his friends, but this time it is one with a twist. Those who seem to be enemies are not, and this book is more concerned with filling in details of Harry's history and character while offering a further mystery for the reader.

14
-
13
-
12
-
11
-
10

Adventure

Magic

School

Wizards

HARRY POTTER AND THE GOBLET OF FIRE
J.K. Rowling
Bloomsbury, 2001, ISBN:0747550999

This book begins with an account of events in the Riddle house and of the Quidditch world cup. At first these seem to have little to do with Harry's progression into fourth year at Hogwarts but the protagonists mentioned in each of these incidents soon prove to be central to the unfolding narrative. The school authorities have decided to reinstate the Triwizard Tournament, a competition between the champions of the three main wizarding schools: Hogwarts, Beauxbatons and Durmstrang. An age barrier should prevent Harry from entering but, mysteriously, his name is also produced from the Goblet of Fire as a competitor. The stage is set for the competition but Harry experiences increasing isolation for the first time at Hogwarts because his friends believe he entered himself for the tournament and failed to include them.

The competition provides an excellent context for the solving of puzzles, the use of initiative and a wide range of magic. However it also provides another opportunity for Voldemort to make a bid to return to power. The outcome of the tournament one might guess, but this, the darkest of the first four novels, provides a sinister atmosphere and further plot development as well as an unexpected and challenging ending. The darkness continues to deepen for an adolescent Harry in *Harry Potter and the Order of the Phoenix* (2003).

THE HAUNTED MOUNTAIN
Mollie Hunter

Armada, 1974 (op); Collins, 1986, ISBN:0006722245 (op)

This story of the haunted mountain is firmly in the folk tradition. It tells of MacAllister, who farmed in a glen some miles from Ben MacDui, and dared the wrath of the fairy folk, the *sidhe*, by reclaiming the 'Goodman's Croft' on his land, the portion traditionally set aside for the fairy folk. MacAllister's revolt against the fairy tradition is a fascinating mixture of a man's proud defiance and his belief in the powers both of Christian faith and the strength of human (and animal) love. Time and again, faith and love enable him to defeat the fairy forces, until finally the former Goodman's Croft becomes the grave of the faithful dog Colm, killed while saving his master from the terrible An Ferla Mor, and survives into the present (according to the narrator) as a garden of healing plants.

This is a novel written for the younger end of the age-range, but has a wide range of appeal.

14
-
13
-
12
-
11
-
10

Celtic tradition

Highlands

Loyalty

PETER AND WENDY
J.M. Barrie

Hodder & Stoughton, 1911 (op); Oxford World's Classics, along with Peter Pan in Kensington Gardens, *1991, ISBN:0192825933. The same story is also published as* Peter Pan *in Puffin Classics, 2002, ISBN:0140366741. Some other editions use the title* Peter Pan and Wendy.

Seven years after the first performance of his 'terrible masterpiece' *Peter Pan*, Barrie published a prose fantasy *Peter and Wendy* which revisits the theme of the boy who refused to grow up. This version incorporates the main dramatic episodes and the best dialogue, but it is much more than the book of the play. It amplifies the absurd comedy of the Darlings' Bloomsbury household; it also explores the alarming world of Peter's Neverland, and finally via Wendy's daughter it returns to the original charged question , 'Boy, why are you crying?' The unique feature of this landmark fiction is the voice of the story-teller. Barrie seems to be speaking conspiratorially to a very young audience about fairies, pirates and redskins. But his language makes few concessions, and the sophisticated tone flits mercurially from wit to sentiment, from parody to melancholy. Is he addressing children or adults or the children within adults, or simply himself? For some the reaction is bound to be confusion, but the work can still offer stimulating entertainment for adventurous young readers. Barrie authorised a simplified edition by May Byron for early school use. BBC Radio Collection has as an abridgement beautifully read by Alan Bennett (2002).

14
-
13
-
12
-
11
-
10

Adventure

Family

Humour

Pirates

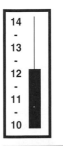

14
-
13
-
12
-
11
-
10

Bullying

Family

Humour

Rivalry

School

PICKING ON PERCY
Cathy MacPhail
Barrington Stoke, 2000, ISBN:1842990594

'O wad some Pow'r the giftie gie us
To see oorsels as ithers see us!'

This dangerous blessing is bestowed on two classmates. Handsome footballer Shawn sees himself as the coolest dude in the school. He enjoys humiliating the wimpish Percy, who has only cheap trainers and enjoys reading. Nightmarishly, after playing a strange new machine in the local amusement arcade, the two lads find that their appearances and circumstances have been totally switched. Shawn looks like, and is treated like Percy, and vice versa. Internally however they retain their self-awareness and realise to their horror what is happening to them. Shawn painfully gains insight into the difficulties of Percy's home life. For his part Percy fits well into Shawn's household but he also misses his own chaotic family. The headmaster, their parents, a newsagent, and the girls in the class are all puzzled by the boys' escapades. The two are finally restored to their original identities, but with a new, wary respect for each other. Neatly told from Shawn's viewpoint the story will be accessible to less confident readers. It should amuse and stimulate 10–12 year-olds.

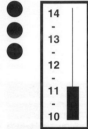

14
-
13
-
12
-
11
-
10

Friendship

Goblins

Love

THE PRINCESS AND THE GOBLIN
George MacDonald
Strahan, 1872, (op); Puffin Classics, 1996, ISBN:0140367462

The level of this extraordinary fantasy is difficult to judge nowadays, for its language is more demanding than the fairy tale nature of the story seems to require. On the other hand it may appear too young for some since the main characters are an eight-year-old girl and a twelve-year-old boy. However the novel is so richly imaginative that it is well worth trying on readers already hooked on Baggins and Potter. The babyish but enterprising Princess Irene, who is kept secluded by her father in a castle in a remote valley, allies with her spectral great-great grandmother and a sturdy boy-miner Curdie to frustrate goblins scheming to abduct her as a bride for their prince Harelip. These Goblins are a wonderfully grotesque subterranean race with no toes and impenetrably hard heads. Their fatal weakness is that they are allergic to rhyme. They are semi-human, malevolent but oddly likeable and their drowning in the final chapter makes grim reading. By the end of the tale Irene attains the stature of a true princess and Curdie is awarded his promised kiss.

STARSHIP RESCUE
Theresa Breslin
Barrington Stoke, 1999, ISBN:1902260902

Young Marc lives on a planet with two suns, which is a very distant colony of Earth. The settlement is ruthlessly controlled by the totalitarian regime of the Keepers whose capital is the Fortress. Privileged citizens, the Chosen Ones, enjoy comfort within its electrified perimeter. The Outsiders by contrast are wretched slave labourers condemned to live in the spoiled wasteland of the Mekonium mines beyond the walls. Because of his agility Marc, who is one of the Outsiders, is selected to trigger a rescue by the Starship Patrol from Earth which cruises past once in every 20 years. His perilous task is to penetrate the Fortress and transmit an SOS message from the Radio Control Station. These efforts are complicated by violent treachery, and he faces the dilemma of deciding who can be trusted. The setting evokes echoes of 1984, concentration camps and the Berlin Wall. This is a short, very effective SF thriller intended for less confident readers and suited to the 10–12 age range. The language is simple with a good deal of dialogue, and tension is well maintained. Issues of tyranny, freedom, betrayal and self-sacrifice are economically suggested.

14
-
13
-
12
-
11
-
10

Outsiders

Space travel

Tyrrany

THE STONE MEN
Murray Herbert
House of Lochar, 2001, ISBN:1899863796

This fantasy is located in the crofting township of Sanna in remotest Ardnamurchan in the 19th century. An old woman recalls strange experiences in her childhood. Lost at night on the shore at Carraig, young Kirsten is abducted into caverns extending under the Minch. This vast domain is inhabited by remnants of Pictish tribes who centuries earlier had gone underground when driven off their lands. They are biding their time to strike back and reclaim their birthright. Eventually Kirsten is released on trust so that she can retrieve the lost stone talisman of the tribes. A struggle of good and evil ensues as the Picts decide the time propitious to break out into the upper world. The fast-moving climax brings a conflict of loyalties for Kirsten. Parallels are hinted between the dispossessed Picts and the cleared crofters of Ardnamurchan. The narrative is intriguing and readable but one odd feature is the invented language attributed to the Picts. While some young readers may find this distracting or comic, it does offer an interesting talking point: how is a novelist to represent dialogue in a lost language?

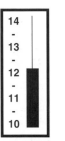

14
-
13
-
12
-
11
-
10

Abduction

Clearances

Picts

Underworld

STRAWGIRL
Jackie Kay
Macmillan, 2002; Macmillan, 2003, ISBN:0330480634

11-year-old Molly MacPherson is nicknamed 'Maybe' because she is temperamentally incapable of making up her mind about anything. This striking venture in magical realism shows how she is transformed into a decisive heroine who saves her mother's Sutherland farm from villainous property developers. The magic emanates from Strawgirl, a bizarre 'corndolly' creature who materialises suddenly when Maybe needs her most, after her Nigerian father's death. Only Maybe can see Strawgirl, who deploys her strange powers to help save the farm. She can make cows fly and trees move; she is both a girl and a force of nature; she hunts and eats mice raw, fears fire and is under the sway of the moon. Under her influence other people begin to recover lost reserves of goodness and strength – a Glasgow hard man, a gang of school bullies and Maybe's own traumatised mother. Like Peter Pan, Strawgirl is a lonely figure who craves human companionship: her final mutation marks the climax of the story. All these elements of magic are balanced by a realistic but touching account of the lives of the MacPhersons' herd of dairy cows. This novel makes demands on young readers' imaginations but it is simply and vividly written.

14 - 13 - 12 - 11 - 10

Animals
Loss
Growing up
Magic
Sutherland

TRAVEL LIGHT
Naomi Mitchison
Faber & Faber, 1952 (op); Virago, 1984, ISBN:0860685624 (op)

This haunting fantasy recounts an enterprising girl's quest for meaning in life. Halla an infant princess in 6th century Novgorod is exposed to die by her stepmother. She is rescued by a bear, and fostered by dragons. She manages to resist the blandishments of the Valkyries but is briefly abducted by brutal robbers. In the course of these escapades she experiences different attitudes to living, and acquires powerful non-human friends and unusual skills. She is for example fireproofed by her dragons, and can speak in all languages and converse with animals. When she encounters a one-eyed stranger, he turns out to be Odin the All-father of Norse religion. Her life is transformed by his quizzical advice, 'Travel light, my child'. As she grows up, her pilgrimage carries her south down the Viking route to the fabled city of Byzantium but the smooth corruption and cruelty of the imperial regime repel her. Heading north again she reluctantly discards her love for the heroic Tarkan Der and soars off into an uncertain future with Steinvor, a disorganised but motherly Valkyrie … travelling light to the end.

Drawing lightly on a wealth of mythology, this novel is by turns witty, lyrical and dramatic. It should present a delightful challenge to confident readers.

14 - 13 - 12 - 11 - 10

Animals
Growing up
History
Mythology
Vikings

WHY WEEPS THE BROGAN?
Hugh Scott
Walker Books, 1989 (op); Walker Books, 1991, ISBN:0744520401 (op)

The reader experiences this disturbing story through the minds of two children, Saxon and her brother Gilbert, whose entire world is the interior of what seems to be a ruinous Victorian museum. The similarities to Glasgow's Kelvingrove are striking. They have been entombed for four years as a result of mysterious 'hostilities'. Growing up in its galleries and ignorant of what may lie outside, they have forgotten their surname and evolved their own obsessive routines of language and behaviour in response to their frightening situation. They live in terror of invasive spiders but cherish the sparrows who colonise the crumbling halls. Above all, they have to cope with an ambiguously monstrous presence which they call The Brogan and which they seem obliged to feed. What or who is The Brogan? The narrative moves swiftly over four days, *Wed to Sat* on the museum's clock. Something of the children's predicament is clarified by a final shift of focus recalling *Lord of the Flies*. Working out the riddle of what has been happening is likely to prove enthralling to young readers. Definitely not for arachnophobes!

14
-
13
-
12
-
11
-
10

Family

Horror

Mystery

THE WIND IN THE WILLOWS
Kenneth Grahame
Methuen, 1908 (op); Penguin, 1994, ISBN:0140621229

Kenneth Grahame, the author of *The Wind in the Willows* was born in Edinburgh in 1859. Shortly afterwards the family moved to Inveraray, Argyll where they remained until 1864 when the children moved to Cookham Dean, a village near the Thames in Berkshire. The novel is set in the world of the River and the Wild Wood. It is peopled by beautifully and carefully observed animals, especially Water Rat, Mole, Badger and Otter, and it particularly focuses on the wonderful adventures of the pompous and selfish Toad who is fascinated by motor cars, steals one and is imprisoned for his crime. He eventually escapes to find that his home Toad Hall has been occupied by stoats and weasels. Thanks to the leadership of Badger the invaders are repelled and normality returns to Toad Hall – although the character of Toad appears to be changed. A wonderfully told story and highly amusing but this is not really an animal novel; rather the animals represent human types. The writer's real purpose seems to be to observe and comment on the English gentry of the upper middle class and the novel is, indeed, an elegy for the old idyllic English rural life which Grahame could see passing away forever. Although the story is straightforward this is a sophisticated work and the language level is challenging for pupils aged 11 to 13.

14
-
13
-
12
-
11
-
10

Allegory

Animals

Humour

Nature

14
-
13
-
12
-
11
-
10

Animals

Growing up

Magic

Outsiders

THE WIND ON THE MOON
Eric Linklater
Macmillan, 1944 (op); Jane Nissen Books, 2000, ISBN:1903252024

We are aware that the phases of the moon are said to influence our lives. Major Palfrey takes this farther and one night sees a wind on the moon which encourages children to behave badly. As soon as he has gone on a long journey his twin daughters Dinah and Dorinda start on a series of wicked adventures, wicked of course only to their hysterical mother and their fact-driven teacher, Miss Serendip. This is a novel about magic. The girls are turned into kangaroos and then seek justice for the inhabitants of the zoo, get their own selves back, trick a judge into setting free a jury he has imprisoned, and finally set off to rescue their father from the castle of a terrible tyrant. They are helped by a witch, talking animals and all kinds of people with funny names. This large book is full of invention and fun, and the pace never flags.

A BRAW BREW
Liz Niven & Pete Fortune (eds)
Watergaw, 1997, ISBN:0952997800

This anthology was specially commissioned to present 'stories in an easily accessible Scots, with modrin, contemporary themes fir weans o 10–14 year auld'. It admirably fulfils its remit, with a range of topics and dictions to appeal to even the most demanding of 14-year-old readers. Janet Paisley in her foreword comments on the *English* bedtime stories that Scots parents read to their children. The collection is designed to give parents and children their own voices back. A wide range of themes and settings is presented. There are fairy tales with a twist, science fiction stories, stories with the traditional theme of the baiting of the neighbouring witch, tales of the recent past and just-disappeared ways of life. The density of Scots tends to increase through the anthology so that familiarity can be built through reading the earlier stories.

Children at the lower end of the age spectrum might find some of these stories rather taxing, as many challenging themes are included, such as the dangers of experimenting with drugs, the onset and consequences of Alzheimer's, the loss of a parent or lifestyle and the inability of a parent to cope with his son's disability. The beauty of the selection is that the stories are so varied and so well arranged that whether the reader starts at page one and reads through to the end, or dips in at random, there is a real sense of variety of tone, language, theme and audience. A terrific anthology.

14 - 13 - 12 - 11 - 10

Adventure

Mystery

Scots language

THE HOOSE O HAIVERS
Matthew Fitt, Susan Rennie, James Robertson
Itchy Coo, 2002, ISBN:1902927443

This delightful and important little book is unique among our recommendations. It takes one of the enduring master works of world literature, Ovid's *Metamorphoses*, and renders some of its best stories in varieties of modern demotic Scots likely to be accessible to young readers. Phaeton for example is a boastful boy racer desperate to drive his father Phoebus's powerful chariot of fire, the 'burnie bogie'. In the end 'he coupit the cairt an syne was fried'. Not all is knockabout however: there is an affecting account of the tragedy of Orpheus in north east Scots. Ranging beyond Ovid the collection offers a hilarious version of 'The Twelve Trauchles o Heracles' in which our hero speaks in the patter of an anarchic hard man exhibiting touches of Rab C. Nesbitt and Desperate Dan. The linguistic vitality of the tales may prove demanding for some who are otherwise competent readers but the answer lies in reading aloud. In places the voice of Ovid speaks directly to his listeners, challenging them about truth, lies, rumours, dreams and storytelling. 'Is it aw a lot o haivers?'

14 - 13 - 12 - 11 - 10

Humour

Mythology

Scots language

LINMILL STORIES
Robert McLellan
Canongate Classics, 1995, ISBN:086241282X

This collection of short stories written in Scots brings together 24 stories originally broadcast on radio between 1960 and 1965. They draw upon McLellan's own childhood memories of holidays on his grandparents' farm in rural Lanarkshire in the earlier years of last century. The topics range widely over aspects of life on and around the farm as observed by a young boy, with the emphasis on the activities and situations that would make the biggest impression on him, such as fishing for minnows, finding a litter of kittens, trapping rabbits, driving a pony and buggy, picking apples, observing the different types of casual farm workers and enduring an old-fashioned Sabbath day. The stories are briskly told from the boy's point of view, with a lot of vivid dialogue, and the personal tone perfectly suits the Scots dialect that runs throughout. The Scots vocabulary and idiom are never obscure because they are used in a clear context, and there is a useful glossary at the end of the book. Most of the stories are well suited in subject and tone for reading aloud to children individually or in a class group, which might extend the appreciation of the stories to slightly younger children. As a Scots language text, this collection can be highly recommended.

Country life

History

Lanarkshire

Scots language

MY MUM'S A PUNK
Theresa Breslin, James McGonigal, Hamish Whyte (eds)
Scottish Children's Press with ASLS, 2002, ISBN:1899827498

This anthology of new Scottish stories and poems touches on themes and conflicts relevant to the lives of its intended readership (10–14), and does so in a lively and engaging way. This derives partly from the different accents heard here, with Ayrshire, Dundonian, Central and Grampian Scots all being represented, and partly from the variety of incident and tone – from school humour and offbeat characters to the puzzlement of coping with difference, personal loss, parents, moral decisions, first love. The instinctive life of domestic and wild animals also features as an entry point to the otherness of nature. This collection's fresh take on issues of Scottish identity is nicely caught in its opening and closing poems that celebrate respectively a punk mum and a gifted girl footballer. (Teaching notes are available from the publishers and on the ASLS website.)

Animals

Growing up

Poetry

School

Scots language

PICTURES IN THE CAVE
George Mackay Brown
Chatto & Windus, 1977 (op); Canongate Kelpies, 1990, ISBN:0862413184 (op)

Sigurd, an imaginative young boy, plays truant and visits the Bay of Seals. Afraid to enter a cave long associated with a terrible witch, Sigurd sits on a rock and watches the basking seals. His subsequent encounter with Shelmark, the seal-boy, provides the framework for a collection of stories based on Orkney legends and key episodes in Scottish history. The cave features in each of the stories and provides a unifying motif. Contrary to local legend, the cave is not cursed but is rather a place of sanctuary.

George Mackay Brown's poetic prose brings to life the legends of the sea and the seal people. The tale of Jennifer Stoor's mysterious disappearance and the poignant story of Cheems, who loved a mermaid, are particularly effective. Other stories are set at various stages in Orkney's history. The people of a Stone Age settlement, forced from their homes by storm and sand, find shelter in the cave. The Vikings create a funeral pyre for their chief and the flames from the cremation create a sail of fire. Other stories link major historical events with the cave. In this collection George Mackay Brown's powerful storytelling creates a magical atmosphere and a distinctive sense of place. The stories are rooted in the legends and history of Orkney but hold a universal appeal.

History
Mythology
Orkney
Supernatural

POINTS NORTH: SHORT STORIES BY SCOTTISH WRITERS
Lindsey Fraser (ed.)
Mammoth, 2000, ISBN:0749740345 (op)

One of the appeals to readers of this anthology is that the contributing writers are as well known (or better known) for their mainstream writing as for their children's stories and novels. These stories are for the very top end of the 10–14 spectrum, and are really stories for teenagers. Some of the contributions are quite challenging, and there are very interesting pairings on similar themes, such as 'Notes in the Margin' by Theresa Breslin and 'Granny's Books' by Gordon Legge, both dealing with the legacy of the past brought into the present in the form of previously unknown personal writings. There are a couple of contrasting stories on the theme of alienation, Julie Bertagna's 'No Ordinary Zombie' and Iain Crichton Smith's 'The Story of Major Cartwright, by Murdo', the first surreal, scary and strange; the second affectionate, slightly mocking and utterly typical of the Iain Crichton Smith-Murdo style. Relationships is a strong theme in the anthology, whether between parents and children as in Dilys Rose's 'These Other Mountains', and Lindsey Fraser's 'Clearing my Head', or among friends as in Jackie Kay's 'The Five Sisters of Kintail'. Kay's blistering account of rivalry amongst a group of teenage girls will strike familiar chords in many readers.

Completing the nine stories are the haunting 'Ghost Track' by Chris Dolan and the enigmatic 'Time Table' by Candia McWilliam. The collection shows how eclectic and indefinable is the term 'Scottish writers'.

Fantasy
Growing up
Relationships
Outsiders

14
-
13
-
12
-
11
-
10

Humour

Mystery

Magic

Scots language

A SCENT OF WATER
Carl MacDougall
Molendinar Press, 1975, ISBN:0904002101 (op)

While based on traditional tales, these 17 stories are originals by Carl MacDougall. They are much longer and more complex than the ones in *A Cuckoo's Nest*. Five of the stories have a hero called Jack and in most of them there is a complex series of adventures or challenges which the hero has to overcome to achieve his goal. The heroes do not always succeed and the book has a healthy down-to-earth realism along with the magic, as all the best folk tales have. Again there is a mixture of traditional rural and modern workplace. The language, however, can be complex – 'speech as witty and wanton as water', 'I'm going tae the bluidy b'roo and I'll raise an erection'. Some jokes have dated too, such as the one where the pretend mechanic thinks a Viva is an Italian car.

The style of this book, however, foreshadows that of MacDougall's first collection of his own stories *Elvis is Dead* and could well serve as an introduction. to these.

14
-
13
-
12
-
11
-
10

Animals

Family

Humour

Outsiders

THE TARTAN RAINBOW
Theresa Breslin (ed.)
Macmillan Children's Books, 2002, ISBN:0330399217

As befits the title, all 14 contributions in this upbeat, varied anthology have happy endings. Mysteries, fears, and tears emerge en route but nothing really horrific occurs. Written by experienced children's authors, these new Scottish stories are accessible and nicely judged in tone for younger readers. Many take the child's eye view and explore the intersecting worlds of adults, children and animals. Animals play a crucial role: pets, wild creatures and young animals, their predicaments mirroring those of the children. Parents, relatives, partners, teachers and other attendant adults are often seen to be inexplicable and ridiculously ineffectual. In Theresa Breslin's 'The Last Box' Josh and Morven observe their respective single parents stumbling comically into a new relationship. Humour is at its most zany in Margaret Ryan's pirates and their parrot, Big Budgie. Frequently the setting is in the Highlands and the context is a holiday. There are outsiders to consider: Alison Prince's English holidaymakers in an Arran village; Julie Bertagna's Muslim asylum seeker in a Glasgow high rise flat; and Jackie Kay's puzzling Orange Man who may be a 'Bad Man' to be avoided, or a benevolent fantasy. This good natured collection presents contemporary dilemmas in a delightfully reassuring fashion.

TWO STORIES: *Wandering Willie's Tale* & *The Two Drovers*
Sir Walter Scott
Canongate, 2001, ISBN:1841951609

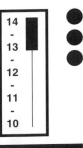

14
-
13
-
12
-
11
-
10

Covenanters

Drovers

Friendship

Horror

Scots language

Supernatural

Despite their appeal to earlier, more docile generations, Sir Walter Scott's novels of adventurous action, eg *Rob Roy* and *Ivanhoe*, are now likely to prove too prolix for even the most committed of younger readers. However, two of his short narratives offer a valuable chance to sample Scott at his most powerful. Both have a supernatural element.

Wandering Willie's Tale (1824): This fearsome account of 'bogle wark' is part of the novel *Redgauntlet* but can stand on its own as a horror story. Steenie Steenson, piper to the diabolical laird of Redgauntlet, arrives at the castle to pay his overdue rent. Thereupon the laird dies in an anguished fit and the money disappears. The drunken Steenie later meets a stranger in the wood who tells him that he must descend to Hell to secure proof that he has actually paid up. He is nearly trapped there but escapes with his receipt, and is able to retrieve the gold coins which the laird's pet monkey had hoarded.

The Two Drovers (1827): In the late 18th century black cattle were driven south from the Highlands to English markets. Robin Oig the drover is a typical John Highlandman, passionately proud of M'Gregor connections and his warrior code of honour. His English companion Harry Wakefield is also seen as a national type, the bluff John-Bull Yorkshireman. Their droving venture from Doune is blighted by the premonitions of a crone reputed to have the Second Sight. When a trivial quarrel between the two flares into a clash of cultures, there is a fatal stabbing, and Robin is condemned to death.

THE WILD RIDE AND OTHER SCOTTISH STORIES
Gordon Jarvie (ed.)
Viking 1986 (op) ; Puffin, 1987, ISBN:0140320350 (op)

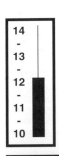

14
-
13
-
12
-
11
-
10

Animals

Family

Growing up

Humour

Supernatural

This generous selection of twentieth century Scottish short stories by well known writers has been chosen with the tastes of younger readers in mind. Most items have youthful protagonists and several are told from their point of view. The emphasis is very much on humour, swinging from knockabout and murderous one-liners to geniality and amusing surprise endings. The perennial puzzles and embarrassments of school days, growing-up and family are treated perceptively. A welcome frisson of the supernatural shivers through yarns such as 'Do you believe in Ghosts?' and 'The Wild Ride in the Tilt Cart'. Animal tales in widely differing moods include accounts of cats, domestic and feral, a pig, a ghost dog and intoxicated geese. One unusual ingredient of the mix is a set of three quite demanding treatments of religious enthusiam: 'Jehovah's Joke', 'Sunday Class' and 'Icarus'. Though the period of this collection stretches back over a couple of generations, and the settings tend to be small-town and rural, it has plenty of the vitality needed to attract young people today.

SPORT

14
-
13
-
12
-
11
-
10

Athletics

Growing up

Humour

Love

Perthshire

GEORDIE
David Walker

Collins, 1950 (op); Nelson, 1991, 0175564671 (op)

Wee Geordie MacTaggart, son a keeper on a Perthshire estate, has climbed a crag to see the chicks in an eagle's eyrie – but he is too small. His little companion Jean, however, *is* tall enough to see them. Geordie, humiliated, subscribes to a body-building course and grows up to become a 'gentle giant'. Specialising in throwing the hammer he achieves remarkable success in the local Highland games, thanks to the inspiration of Jean, now his sweetheart. After this he finds himself selected for the Olympic Games in USA. Whilst there he rescues the victim of a car accident and the American people take him to their hearts. On the day of his event he is in poor form. At the last minute, however, in his imagination he sees Jean cheering him on and wins to the delight of the crowd – and Helga, the Danish shot putt champion who embraces him passionately in public. Geordie comes home to a cold reception and has to pacify a furious Jean. The character of the young, innocent but thrawn Highlander who embodies the timeless theme of the puny youngster aspiring to physical perfection is nicely drawn. The book's other triumph is the portrait of the wonderfully eccentric local laird.

14
-
13
-
12
-
11
-
10

Crofting

Family

Shinty

Skye

THE SHINTY BOYS
Margaret MacPherson

Collins, 1963 (op); Collins, 1975, ISBN:0006709966 (op)

Young Neillie and his friends live in a Skye township. They are fanatical about shinty but learn to their dismay that they must lose their school team unless they can find money to keep it going. Despising the cheaper alternative of football they devote their summer holiday to fund-raising. Their enterprise and misadventures throw light realistically on crofting life in the late 1950s. The boys desperately try to earn cash while doing their normal summer chores, tending cattle, stacking peats, cutting bracken, feeding the hens, helping caravanners. The austere limitations of their lives are lightly signalled. Neillie's pious father is brutal at times and Sunday observance seems irksome. On the other hand the shinty hero Uncle Angus is sympathetic, and day-long communion is balanced by the guilty delights of the Portree Games. Relatives on holiday from London complicate their efforts. The boys succeed unexpectedly at the last minute and when school resumes they are nursing ambitions of growing up to win the Camanachd Cup. This stimulating summer story offers a good pairing with *The Battle of Wednesday Week*.

THE BOGGART
Susan Cooper
Puffin, 1993, ISBN:0140364889

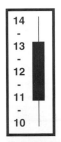

14
13
12
11
10

Argyll

Canada

Computers

Humour

Spirit mischief

A boggart is 'kin to a brownie, a house spirit of no malice but endless mischief'. They are shape shifters, found exclusively in Scotland and Northern England. This boggart resides in Castle Keep, Port Appin, Argyll, the home of The MacDevon. The old man has lived for over a hundred years, largely in harmony with the boggart, each indulging the other by tricking and being tricked. When The MacDevon dies the Volnik family inherit Castle Keep and come from Canada to see their inheritance. The castle is sold and some of the furniture transported to Canada along with the boggart who has gone to sleep in a roll-top desk – which he can't escape because he is unable to cross doors with iron locks.

When he finally escapes the boggart is entranced with the world in which he finds himself and causes all kinds of mischief until he finally causes a problem with serious consequences. As far as the boggart is concerned his mischief has an escalating scale and a clear purpose: he will keep the family from getting bored and they will, on the whole, enjoy him. The children find out about the boggart just as he is becoming homesick. They have to find a way of transporting him back to Scotland. The ingenious solution involves computers and computer games and offers an interesting contrast of the ultra-modern, hi-tech world with the old traditional one.

THE BOGGART AND THE MONSTER
Susan Cooper
Bodley Head, 1998; Puffin, 2000, ISBN:0141302070

14
13
12
11
10

Family

Humour

Nessie

Spirit mischief

Events have moved on two years since the first book and the Volnik family return to Scotland on holiday. The new owner of Castle Keep has discovered, by bitter experience, about the boggart. Gradually it emerges that the Canadian children and Tommy, a local boy, know about him too. They all go off on a camping trip to Loch Ness taking along the boggart who has become trapped in a tent. There the boggart discovers a long lost cousin, Nessie, who is also a boggart but has forgotten how to change shape.

The rest of the tale is tells how the children and the boggart attempt to free Nessie from Loch Ness to allow him to re-learn his shape-shifting skills and to live in closer proximity to his cousin. The attempts by the monster to sustain a shape which will allow him to move without being seen provide much of the book's humour, and are thwarted by all kinds of natural disasters. The children have to help the boggart maintain his shape with their minds and get caught up in a car accident, and by journalists in pursuit of a story. The writing is such that it is very easy to achieve a 'willing suspension of disbelief' and the references to scientific events and inventions, historical events, myths and legends add to the rich texture of the tale.

14
-
13
-
12
-
11
-
10

Magic

Mystery

Nature

Quest

The sea

CREATURES OF THE CARP
Ronald Portchmouth
Scottish Children's Press, 1998, ISBN:189982765X

This extraordinary story of mystery and magic is set in a remote fishing community somewhere in the wild north coast of Scotland, caught between the powerful forces of the sea and the dark mysteries of a rocky headland. The promontory, known as the Carp, is the source of many strange tales, mysterious disappearances, unearthly creatures, sounds and shapes in the shadows. When a shepherd accidentally discovers there an old book full of obscure words and symbols, powerful forces are unleashed. As a result young Rory, the hero, finds himself caught up in a quest to solve a puzzle and defeat evil. The novel's characters are archetypal: the orphan children, the evil old man who seeks the power of magic for selfish and evil ends, and the greedy neighbours; it also contains many fairy tale elements such as magical transformations and incredible escapes. But above all we are left with a strong sense that there is much more to this world than meets the eye. Setting and atmosphere are powerfully realised, the supernatural is convincing and the storyline keeps the reader gripped.

14
-
13
-
12
-
11
-
10

Family

Growing up

Moving house

Psychic powers

THE GARGOYLE
Hugh Scott
Walker Books, 1991 (op); Walker Books, 1992, ISBN:0744523303

Like all the best horror stories this contemporary spine-chiller is farfetched but persuasively crafted. It is set among the atmospheric splendours of a group of dilapidated Victorian villas, seemingly those of Cove along the shore of Loch Long. The Kent family have just moved up from London on father's appointment to a Chair in Glasgow University. Their teenage daughter Marion is burdened with alarming psychic powers which she is determined to keep under responsible control. To her dismay she quickly senses that while her new home has a benign aura, baleful emanations are seeping in from nearby. The weather is freezing cold; ominously the phone line is down, and a bizarre death occurs almost immediately. Grotesque nocturnal things are on the move as a confused struggle develops between youthful goodness and adult malignity. The novel catches the domestic excitements of moving into an unfamiliar house and meeting new neighbours. It also conveys subtleties of parent and child relationships. The author has an artist's eye for original detail and startling images. If young readers keep their wits about them, and their nerve, they will enjoy this very challenging read.

GHOST AT THE WINDOW
Margaret McAllister
Oxford University Press, 2000, ISBN:0192718479

Young Ewan and his parents have moved to Ninian House, a remote place on a Galloway lochside, and have come to accept their new home's habit of switching on sporadic glimpses of its long history. Life becomes troubled for Ewan when he discovers that his bedroom is haunted by 7-year-old Elspeth who is begging his help. In 1937 she had been on the point of dying with diphtheria when the house had in one of its momentary time-shifts locked her, 'sort of dead', in a mysterious borderland. She yearns to be released finally into the lovely music which will bring a peaceful closure to her life. The novel describes Ewan's quest to free her from her time-trap. Even as ghost stories go, this has an improbably complex resolution involving a symbolic lion and a cupboard, though no witch! It is marked by attractive characterisation of the sensible Ewan and his preoccupied, artistic parents. Sadness and humour mingle in the relationships of the boy and the girl who find themselves, across 60 years, sharing the same bedroom. An original, thought-provoking tale for confident readers.

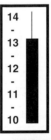

14 - 13 - 12 - 11 - 10

Family
Galloway
Ghosts
History

THE KELPIE'S PEARLS
Mollie Hunter
Blackie, 1964 (op); Floris Kelpies, 1993, ISBN:0862414431

Set in the hills above Loch Ness, near the isolated croft where old Morag MacLeod lives contentedly alone, this story neatly reveals the conflicting claims of three worlds. Morag's traditional Highland way of life is disrupted by the modern world of media, tourism and greed (represented mainly by Alasdair the Trapper), but it is also disturbed by the uncanny world of the supernatural, in the form of the cunning water kelpie whom she comes to know, and in her final desperate use of the spell-book of her grandmother, locally renowned as a witch. Morag's true friend is the orphaned lad, Torquil, himself gifted in the taming of animals. Alasdair the Trapper plots to dam the burn that feeds the pool where the kelpie's pearls are hidden. He is foiled when Morag conjures up a 3 day storm. This is vividly described, as are the Loch Ness monster's apparition, and Morag's final ride on a black steed, through death to the Land of Eternal Youth.

14 - 13 - 12 - 11 - 10

Highlands
Nessie
Spirits
Witches

14
-
13
-
12
-
11
-
10

Edinburgh

Family

Friendship

Ghosts

Thriller

THE MARTLET BOX
Jean Ross
Canongate, 1987 (op); Floris Kelpies, 1990, ISBN:0862412803

Cousins Simon and Malcolm soon discover that being sent to stay with their Great Uncle Henry in Edinburgh turns out to be far from boring. They and their friend Robina become caught up in a fantastic and timeless battle between the forces of light and darkness for possession of the magical martlet box. Helped by the beautiful, immortal Mrs Clarke they must firstly elude and outwit the ghostly Captain who haunts them like a dark shadow. Next they must help undo the trouble caused when Great Uncle and Gran had come into possession of the box as children during a strange journey back in time down the narrow misty wynds of old Edinburgh. Finally they must undertake a perilous quest to save Robina's soul and prevent the box from falling into the clutches of the sinister Captain. Although the language is demanding in places this is a haunting ghost story and exciting mystery which succeeds in making the supernatural fantasy quite credible.

14
-
13
-
12
-
11
-
10

Argyll

Divorce

Family

Growing up

PANTHER IN ARGYLL
Lisa Tuttle
Mammoth 1996, (op); Mammoth 2000, ISBN:0749744790

Yet another summer adventure in Scotland, but with a grim difference. The narrator, a teenager with attitude, is shunted off on holiday to her godmother, who edits a local newspaper in Argyll. Later she discovers that her parents are separating. In moving from Birmingham to the disturbing territory that lies beyond the Rest-and-Be-Thankful, Danni discovers that she has 'a gift with a dark side', a capacity to morph almost at will into the identity of a wild panther. The mood of the narrative, with its bloody details of animal slaughter, owes much to the American psycho creepiness of the popular Point Horror fiction series. It plays also on the werewolf myth and echoes of Jekyll and Hyde. Some of the key figures are incomers who are trying to leave behind troubles from elsewhere. In more than one sense stalking is a theme. A strength lies in the intensity of the mutating relationship between Danni and her prowling friend Fin. Some may find the panther kills hard to stomach but this bizarre, disconcerting narrative is likely to appeal to many young readers.

ROBINSHEUGH
Eileen Dunlop

Oxford University Press, 1975 (op); Richard Drew, 1987, ISBN:0862671949 (op)

Like most of Dunlop's novels, this takes as its premise that this world is connected to the past through places. Elizabeth Martin's aunt is researching the Melville family papers at Robinsheugh, and has little time or inclination to entertain her twelve-year-old niece. Elizabeth finds a looking glass which translates her into the body and mind of Elizabeth Melville, who lived in the house two hundred years before. Although she cannot control her time travel, and does not understand how it is that no-one realises she is not Elizabeth Melville, Elizabeth Martin cannot stop herself using the mirror to go to the nursery where she is loved and valued. An interesting feature of plot construction is that Elizabeth is aware most of the time of who she actually is, and she has to learn how to act as her eighteenth century self, but the transformation becomes more dangerously real and threatening until Elizabeth Martin faces a real risk of losing her own mind and personality.

There is a fascinating ongoing discussion of the differences between our world and that of the past, a questioning of modern and past mores, and an examination of the relationships between children and adults, which may be quite challenging for younger children.

14
-
13
-
12
-
11
-
10

Borders
Family
History
Relationships

THE THIRTEENTH MEMBER
Mollie Hunter

Hamish Hamilton, 1971, Floris Kelpies, 2002, ISBN:0863154050

The story of Gilly, the thirteenth member of the North Berwick coven, consecrated to the coven by her mother when she was a baby. Adam Lawrie, the bondservant who discovers her secret is the only one she can rely on to help her escape the witches and save the king, James VI, from their treasons. Adam and Gilly witness the witches plotting to kill the king by using a waxen model which they will cast into the flames, and then Adam has the terrifying experience of seeing Gilly participate in a sabbat where the devil appears on a horse flowing with fire. This is essential evidence that they can only present to the king, James VI – itself a very dangerous undertaking, especially in Gilly's situation. Dr Fian, the notorious leader of the coven, and Agnes Sampson, the leading female witch, undergo the most horrific tortures to make them confess to the king, and Gilly herself does not escape the thumbscrews and the rope.

Although quite a short novel, this is dense and complex, and not suitable for readers under 12. It is fascinating to set Hunter's version against the contemporary account, to look at issues of language, religious belief and justice.

14
-
13
-
12
-
11
-
10

History
Loyalty
Witches

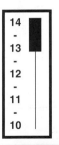

WHISPERS IN THE GRAVEYARD
Theresa Breslin
Methuen, 1994 (op); Mammoth, 2000, ISBN:0749744804

A gripping tale centred on the dyslexic Solomon, ridiculed and persecuted by his teacher, abandoned by his mother and threatened by his father's uncontrolled drinking bouts. Solomon regularly bunks off school and spends his time in the local graveyard, but when plans are made to dig up and relocate the tombs, the horrors of the past begin to come to light. Solomon's highly developed imagination opens his mind to the evil in the graveyard, and he gradually realises that past events are controlling the present and drawing in both Solomon himself, and Amy, the daughter of the scientist called in to advise the council. Only the strategies that Solomon has adopted to shut himself off from the impossibilities of the classroom give him the strength to defeat the powers of the seventeenth century witch out for revenge for her burning.

Breslin writes in a vivid, naturalistic style, but with a poetic undertone, evoking the stories of fantasy and supernatural that Solomon's father related to him and which bonded the two of them so closely.

THE WITCH OF LAGG
Anne Pilling
Lions, 1985; Collins, 2000, ISBN:0007102690

Another variation on the theme of holiday escapades in Scotland. Colin and Prill are stuck in a gloomy castle with their irritating cousin Oliver who has an abnormal capacity for sensing the presence of evil in his surroundings. When inadvertently they release a spirit from the past, there follow poltergeist manifestations, an incubus, foul miasmas, sudden appearances of blood and other baleful signs. Harmony is restored only after a forest fire has purged the reclusive and terrifying laird of Lagg of the malevolence that haunts him. This is a horror story which takes melodramatic liberties with the 17th century witchcraft and religious persecutions in Galloway and particularly with traditions of the drowned martyrs of Wigtown and the merciless Grierson of Lagg. It belongs to the lurid genre of gothic fantasy with which many young readers undoubtedly enjoy scaring themselves. The weird adventures of Oliver and the Bateman family feature also in *Black Harvest* (1999) and *The Beggar's Curse* (2000). Confident readers might like to progress to the macabre account of diablerie in 'Wandering Willie's Tale' to be found in Sir Walter Scott's *Two Stories* (see p.69).

HUNTINGTOWER
John Buchan
Hodder & Stoughton, 1922 (op); Oxford Classics, 1998, ISBN: 0192837214

Moving between Glasgow and South-West Scotland, this novel introduces the recently retired grocer Dickson McCunn and the Gorbals Die-Hards. McCunn is an unlikely hero embarking on a quiet walking tour in Carrick to celebrate his retirement, and the Die-Hards, led by the resourceful Dougal, are a group of adolescents too poor to join the official Boy Scouts of the time. With high ideals the boys are seeking adventure and they find it in the remote coastal village of Dalquharter on the border of Ayrshire and Galloway where stands the mysterious house of Huntingtower. McCunn and the Diehards gain an unexpected ally in the shape of the Poet as they attempt to rescue from captivity and the dark forces of Bolshevism a Russian princess, her companion and her treasure. The narrative, although perhaps a little dated, is exciting and well-organised from the quiet beginning to the final, violent confrontation. Its themes of heroism, independence, loyalty and co-operation remain relevant today. Much use is made of dialogue, mainly in a convincing Scots; the setting in time and place is expertly created, and the characterisation worked through with conviction.

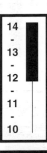

14
-
13
-
12
-
11
-
10

Adventure

Espionage

Glasgow

Scots language

South-west

JOHN MACNAB
John Buchan
Hodder & Stoughton, 1925 (op); Wordsworth, 1996, ISBN:185326296X

To relieve their summer boredom in London, three figures in public life – a lawyer, a banker, and a statesman – decide to seek adventure in Scotland by poaching, using only sporting methods, a stag and a salmon from the estates of their friend's neighbours. Success or failure will be met with donations to charity; all they risk are their public reputations, although the challenge is issued under the nom de guerre of John Macnab. To complicate matters, one of the central characters has just been adopted as a prospective parliamentary candidate for the constituency. There is a wide cast of characters, from the local enterprising urchin to the pompous laird. Buchan draws on all his knowledge of Highland sporting life to create a convincing background which will appeal to readers with an interest in these areas. This is an engaging tale of wit and humour and there is no little excitement as the protagonists pursue their aims, their feelings changing as their adventures succeed or fail. Much of the narrative is described in military terms, a device entirely consistent with the characters and the plot.

14
-
13
-
12
-
11
-
10

Adventure

Fishing

Highlands

Humour

Hunting

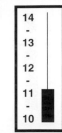

14
-
13
-
12
-
11
-
10

Adventure

Crime

Hillcraft

Nature

Stirlingshire

LIGHT ON DUMYAT
Rennie McOwan

Saint Andrew Press, 1982 (op); Saint Andrew Press, 2001, ISBN:0715206974

Disappointed that the family holiday on Anglesey has been cancelled Gavin agrees to his mother's suggestion that he visit his Scottish relatives, Uncle Fergus and Aunt Elspeth who live in a rambling mansion in the countryside near Stirling. When he arrives there he explores Dumyat, the most westerly peak of the Ochil Hills, and while doing so meets up with the Clan, three children from a nearby farm. Gavin expresses a wish to join the Clan but to do this he is required to pass a test which involves avoiding detection by the Clan in a specified area over a twenty-four hour period. While this is going on a gang of thieves capture his Uncle Fergus, his housekeeper and eventually Gavin too. Fergus has been re-searching a book on Scottish silverware and he has been lent a collection of very valuable pieces by a museum. The thieves are on the point of making off with this when the Clan intervenes and in an exciting conclusion the rogues are captured. The narrative is vivid and quick moving and the characters clear and uncompli-cated. The reader is also cleverly introduced to interesting aspects of hillcraft and wildlife. The adventures continue in *The White Stag Adventure* and *The Day the Mountain Moved*.

14
-
13
-
12
-
11
-
10

Edinburgh

History

Jacobites

Smuggling

THE LOTHIAN RUN
Mollie Hunter

Canongate, 1984 (op); Floris Kelpies, 2003, ISBN:0863154131

Set in Edinburgh in 1736, and dealing with the twin plots of smuggling through Fife and preparations for a second Jacobite rising, this is typical Hunter territory, non-stop action from the outset.

The central character is 16 year-old Sandy, who is apprenticed to lawyer Wishart, but bored with being stuck in the dusty legal office. When he meets Deryck Gilmour, the rather glamorous but always sharp and pragmatic Special Investigator for HM Customs, Sandy learns that the law can be an exciting pro-fession. Gilmour is on the track of a smuggler, George Robertson, who has robbed a Customs post, but with Sandy's help he finds that he is connected with the mercenary St Clair, who is raising a cavalry force to lead a second Jacobite rising. When Robertson steals St Clair's military despatch, intending to use it as a bar-gaining counter if he should be taken, the two plots coincide, and Sandy and Gilmour find themselves in the crossfire.

Rather reminiscent of *Kidnapped* in its chases across rough land, its frequent short gun-fights and the sense of very real danger that is created, this is a gripping read, culminating in the Porteous riot, where the mob lynch the former Captain of the Town Guard.

MURDO'S WAR
Alan Temperley
Canongate Kelpies, 1990, ISBN:0862413168

This adventure story is set in Caithness in 1943. Murdo, the 14-year-old protagonist helps out his family by working with Hector, an old rogue of a fisherman: his father is in the army. Hector is involved in smuggling whisky from Orkney for the black market. Hector and Murdo undertake a new job for Mr Henry Smith: supposedly they are moving vital new engine parts. Murdo has some suspicions about the contents and one night he discovers they are actually guns and grenades destined for a covert German invasion of Britain.

Suddenly Murdo is plunged headlong into a deep and dangerous adventure of national proportions. Murdo manages to escape, intent on getting the vital information to the police or army and to thwart the potential disaster. There follows a deadly hunt across Scotland's harshest terrain, from Strathy Point to Helmsdale, in the depth of winter. Can Murdo outwit the enemy before Operation Flood-Tide can be set in motion?

Murdo's War is an exciting story of guns, boat and car chases, evasions and mountain pursuits. The descriptive writing is powerful and evocative – and the level of suspense is sustained and exciting. The novel is reminiscent in many ways of John Buchan's World War I tale *The Thirty-Nine Steps* with its long pursuit across the moor, and may have particular appeal for male readers.

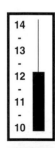

14
-
13
-
12
-
11
-
10

Caithness

Espionage

War

World War II

SIMON'S CHALLENGE
Theresa Breslin
Canongate, 1988 (op), Floris Kelpies, 2002, ISBN:0863154085

Ideal for top primary or early secondary, the novel covers a number of contemporary themes: redundancy, and the related poverty it causes; a threatened marriage breakdown; sibling relationships and the parent's expectations of the elder sibling; crime and retribution/reward. Simon is the unwitting witness of the robbery from Paterson's computer shop, where he spends much of his spare time testing the new games for the owner. It is his dream to have a computer of his own, but his father's redundancy (a concept which is dealt with particularly well in the novel) means that there is no money to spare. He has a number of challenges to face, but the ultimate, and that of the title, is the challenge to remember the relevant facts about the night of the robbery, in order to enable the police to catch the robber. Inevitably he does, and his reward is a top-of-the-range computer.

Breslin's style is contemporary and streetwise without being easily dated, and her characters ring very true to life.

14
-
13
-
12
-
11
-
10

Computers

Crime

Family

Unemployment

14
-
13
-
12
-
11
-
10

Espionage

Galloway

Patriotism

World War I

THE THIRTY-NINE STEPS
John Buchan
Blackwood, 1915 (op); Oxford World Classics, 1999, ISBN:0192839314

This tale of derring-do, murder, patriotism and espionage is set immediately before the First World War. The hero is a mining engineer Richard Hannay, who also figures in later Buchan novels. Recently returned from South Africa he is a resourceful but dour open-air type who feels out of place in London society. When he finds a man murdered in his London flat and is pursued by police and foreign spies, he flees to Scotland to work out the significance of the victim's notebook and of the mysterious 'thirty-nine steps'. Through unlikely but convincing situations he manages – sometimes only just – to stay ahead of the pursuit until he succeeds in foiling his adversary, a brilliant German master spy.

This is an enthralling chase novel full of incident, intrigue and cliff-hanging moments. The characters are not stereotyped although the heroes are heroic and the villains villainous enough. The complex plot is carefully organised, with a sensitive feeling for place, especially for the remoter parts of Galloway and southern Scotland. The underlying mood is of foreboding as civilisation is threatened by imminent global conflict.

BROONIES, SILKIES & FAIRIES: TRAVELLERS' TALES
Duncan Williamson

Canongate, 1985, 1993, ISBN:0862414563 (op)

This is another collection of stories told by Duncan Williamson, whose store of folktales comes out of his origins and upbringing as one of the travelling people in the first half of the twentieth century. The stories focus on the traditional lore of brownies, fairies and seal-people. The Brownie stories illustrate the idea of the benevolent helpful spirit in the form of a little old man who intervenes in people's lives to demonstrate the importance of kindness and practical goodness. The Fairies in the stories, however, are more dangerous. They should not be crossed or betrayed, and they have a habit of taking people or children away to their own realm. The stories of the Silkies depend on the ability of the seal-people to live either on land as humans or in the water as seals yet always in the end having to return to their true home in the sea. The style of the stories is clear and colloquial, with some use of Scots words and expressions; there is a helpful short glossary at the end. The collection can be highly recommended especially for reading aloud.

14 - 13 - 12 - 11 - 10

Scots language

Supernatural

Travelling folk

A CUCKOO'S NEST
Carl MacDougall

Molendinar Press, 1974, ISBN:0904002047 (op)

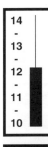

The subtitle says that this book contains 'lesser known Scottish folk tales collected and retold by Carl MacDougall'. The collection would be suitable for readers whose attention span is brief but who like challenging ideas. The 23 stories, from under one page to four pages in length, are widely varied in content, and come from a range of places in Scotland. As well as traditional accounts of romantic forests and Highlands there are some retellings of urban myths. Thus we have tales of seals, princesses and ghosts but also that of the apprentice sent to get the left-handed screw driver. Many have the quality of humorous riddles, and would encourage discussion. The style is straightforward, and intriguing complexities in the narrative are carefully explained step by step.

14 - 13 - 12 - 11 - 10

Animals

Fantasy

Humour

Nature

14
13
12
11
10

Fantasy

Supernatural

Travelling folk

FIRESIDE TALES OF THE TRAVELLER CHILDREN
Duncan Williamson

Canongate, 1983 (op); Canongate, 1995, ISBN: 0862410479 (op)

The stories in this collection are told in the words of Duncan Williamson, a noted source of the Scottish folklore tradition preserved within the community of travelling people through the first half of the twentieth century. They are stories told to the children at bedtime, and deal with wonderful magical events involving kings and princesses and travelling people, witches and fairies and enchanted animals. The settings are familiar folktale places very like rural Scotland of 'once upon a time'. Because the stories were told to an audience of young people, they are direct and easy to read. The collection has an introduction describing the travelling way of life and how the children of travelling families used to grow up; there are interesting notes at the end of the book on the origin and style of each story. These stories can be thoroughly recommended for either reading by children or reading aloud to them.

14
13
12
11
10

Borders

Fantasy

History

Reivers

Supernatural

THE GOLD OF FAIRNILEE
Andrew Lang

J W Arrowsmith, 1888 (op); in Scottish Folk and Fairy Tales, *edited Gordon Jarvie; Penguin Popular Classics, 1997, ISBN:0140622063*

This 50 page Victorian tale gently sanitises Tam Lin, a fierce ballad of fairy transformations. It suits a younger audience than Mitchison's *The Big House*, which exploits the same folk material. Lang's voice is that of the storyteller quietly recalling and glossing an old story for his listeners. He is coyly apologetic in his infrequent use of Border Scots, but there is an authentic feeling for the reivers' territory of Yarrow, Ettrick and Tweed. The period is the ill years after the battle of Flodden. Jean, an orphan accidentally brought back from a raid into England, is raised as a ward of the Kerrs of Fairnilee. Her steadfast goodness in the ordeal of Midsummer Night redeems the young laird, Randall, from seven years' imprisonment and impending sacrifice in the dark realm of the Fairy Queen. Helped by their old nurse the two employ a strange fluid from fairyland as a metal-detector to unearth a hoard of Roman gold. This trove they put to selfless use in rescuing their land from famine.

THE GREEN MAN OF KNOWLEDGE
Alan Bruford

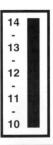

14
-
13
-
12
-
11
-
10

Aberdeen University Press, 1982, ISBN:0080257585 (op)

This collection of tales consists of pieces of oral tradition collected from the Borders to the Northern Isles. The storytellers include Jack Cockburn (Berwickshire), Jeannie and Stanley Robertson (Aberdeenshire), and Tom Tulloch (Shetland). All items are in varieties of Scots. The most interesting feature of this volume is the inclusion of a number of international wonder tales (*märchen*) 'which most people in this country expect to have been translated from another language' but have now become part of our own tradition. This tale type has usually been associated with Gaelic folk tradition but in recent years a vigorous stream of Scots *märchen* has been recovered from the travelling people. They form the core of this volume. 'One-Eye, Two-Eyes, Three-Eyes' is a version of the Cinderella story. 'Jack and the Devil's Purse' is a reversal of the Faust legend. The long 'The Green Man of Knowledge' with its simpleton hero Jack and its talking animals is a version of the international type *The Girl as Helper in the Hero's Flight*. There are also some wonderfully eerie stories, dramatically told, about the devil and death such as 'The Devil at the Foul Ford' and 'The Angel of Death' and some humorous and tall tales. These stories, in their racy Scots, will be more effective if they are read confidently to a class. They can be enjoyed – and discussed in considerable depth – across the whole age range.

Fantasy

Supernatural

Scots language

A KIST O' WHISTLES
Moira Miller

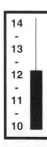

14
-
13
-
12
-
11
-
10

Andre Deutsch, 1990; Mammoth, 1992, ISBN:0749709464 (op)

This delightful collection offers accessible, lively versions of 11 Scottish folk and fairy tales including classic themes such as The Seal Wife, Silly Jack, The Puddock Princess, Michael Scott and Coinneach Odhar. They come from places as far apart as Orkney, Galloway and Skye, and the centrepiece is a finely worked rendering of Rashiecoat. Although lightly coloured by modern allusions, these are clear retellings of the traditional tales. They are crafted literary pieces rather than oral transcripts but a strongly distinctive storyteller's voice is nonetheless present: informal, humorous, gossipy and involving. There is confident use of colloquial Scots dialogue. The tone is mainly lighthearted, with baddies such as the wee folk, the giant's wife and the imp o' hell being shown as comically antisocial, hyperactive or simply dim. One tale, 'The Stealing of Christie McHarg', is more grimly frightening, and the sadness of 'The Seal Wife' is delicately conveyed.

The stories call out for dramatic activities, use of tape recorders and students' own efforts at storytelling. Supporting stimuli are available in the enticing illustrations by Mairi Hedderwick.

Humour

Supernatural

Scots language

14
-
13
-
12
-
11
-
10

Celtic tradition

Fantasy

Highlands

Love

Supernatural

THE MOUTH OF THE NIGHT
Iris Macfarlane
Chatto & Windus, 1973 (op); Puffin 1977, ISBN:0140308814 (op)

This collection of fourteen folk tales is taken from the famous volumes of *Popular Tales of the West Highlands* (1860-2) collected and translated from Gaelic by the celebrated folklorist and polymath John Francis Campbell of Islay. Iris Macfarlane has re-translated her selection 'trying to alter as little as possible, but of necessity softening, and sorting and linking' in order to make them suitable for young children. These are international wonder tales full of impossible tasks, spells, kings and queens, evil witches, ugly monsters, massive giants, talking animals and magic islands. 'The Sharp Grey Sheep' is a wonderful version of the Cinderella story. 'The Sea Maiden' tells the tale of the old fisherman who is promised successful catches if he is prepared to give up his son to the sea maiden. 'The Brown Bear of the Green Glen' is a story of jealousy. The king's youngest son sustains great dangers to fetch special water from the Green Isle on the edge of the world which will cure his father's illness. On his return he is ambushed by his jealous brothers who want the glory of his achievement. He becomes ill and disfigured but is finally identified by his wife, the brothers are punished and all ends happily. Iris Macfarlane's vivid translation does justice to these texts from oral tradition. The frequent recounting of events in groups of three and the repetition of lengthy passages come across as natural and effective. Given their nature these stories will be more attractive and compelling to children if they are read aloud.

14
-
13
-
12
-
11
-
10

Fantasy

Humour

Supernatural

THE WELL AT THE WORLD'S END
Norah and William Montgomerie
Hogarth Press, 1956 (op); Floris Kelpies, 2002, ISBN:0862414628

For younger readers this collection of 35 brief stories is the best source for simple versions of the classic folk tales of Scotland. They come from all parts, Highland, Island and Lowland: 'Whuppity Stoorie' (Dumfries), 'The Goodman of Wastness' (Orkney), 'The Smith and the Fairies' (Islay), 'Jock and his Bagpipes' (Fife), 'Finn and the Grey Dog' (Argyll) and many more. These renderings are clear and basic, discarding the idioms of the oral storyteller. Sadly the authors felt obliged to translate Scots dialects into English. Though contracted in length they are far from prettified in content. They deal with giants, talking animals, mermaids, cannibalism, heroes, gold and silver hoards, clever girls who marry the King's son, and menacing powers such as the Stove Worm, and the King of Elfland. Overall they retain some primitive strangeness from their originals, vigorous but occasionally unfeeling or downright savage. Norah Montgomerie's delightful drawings are much gentler than the disconcerting stories they illustrate. This collection is for dipping into but it can also offer stimulus for drama, art and music in school. Recordings of oral storytelling in Scots are available on the CD *Scottish Traditional Tales* (Greentrax, 2000).

AUTHOR INDEX

TITLE INDEX

KEYWORDS INDEX

87